Encountering God and Discovering Our True Identity

John Littleton

Encountering God and Discovering Our True Identity

Reflections on the First Readings of Cycle A

the columba press

First published in 2013 by
the columba press
55A Spruce Avenue, Stillorgan Industrial Park,
Blackrock, Co. Dublin

Cover design by Leeann Gallagher, The Columba Press
Cover artwork: *An Open Invitation* (Glenstal Abbey) by Gerry Carew
Origination by The Columba Press
Printed in Ireland by SPRINT-Print Ltd

ISBN 978 1 78218 115 6

Contents

Preface

The main purpose of this book is to provide readers with a greater appreciation of the lectionary's first readings – mostly, but not exclusively, chosen from the Old Testament (the Hebrew scriptures) – which are proclaimed during Year A of the church's three-year liturgical cycle. A series of reflections on the readings is presented for each Sunday and for selected solemnities and feast days.

The reflections focus on the crucial significance of the word of God, and on its life-giving and liberating message for everyday life. They will be helpful to clergy and laity wishing to engage more fully with the sacred scriptures, and will be especially useful for preachers and members of prayer groups, Bible-study classes and *lectio divina* gatherings preparing for the celebration of the Liturgy of the Word on the various Sundays and feast days. An appendix catalogues in alphabetical order the specific chapters and verses from the biblical books that comprise the first readings for the Sundays of the year. A concise glossary is also provided.

Before each reflection, the scripture reference for the relevant reading is listed. Then after the reflection, a suitable phrase from the reading is offered as an aid to meditation. Lastly, the alternative opening prayer for the Mass on the particular Sunday or feast day is provided. The prayers, which are quite beautifully composed, are taken from the English translation of the second typical edition of *The Roman Missal*, which formally ceased being used for the celebration of Mass on the First Sunday of Advent in 2011.

As suggested by the book's title, it is essentially when we experience and meet God in many different but interconnected ways – but especially when we listen to and ponder the inspired word of God – that we discover and reaffirm our true identity. Being made in the image and likeness of God, that identity originates in God and guides us throughout this earthly life as we journey back to God.

The scripture quotations throughout the book are taken from the *Jerusalem Bible* because that is the version of the scriptures that is generally included in lectionaries (with the exception of the psalms, which are taken from the Grail version) and, as such, the version with which most people are familiar. Unfortunately, however, the *Jerusalem Bible* does not always employ gender-inclusive language. Also, when reading or speaking, it is customary, as a sign of profound reverence, it is customary not to pronounce the sacred name 'YHWH', which is a transliteration of the proper name by which the God of Israel is known; 'the Lord' is the most commonly used substitution.

Although the reflections may be read without necessarily referring to the readings, it is recommended that readers also consult their bibles or missals. Otherwise, individual scriptural phrases could easily be taken out of context. Also, because the word of God is inexhaustible, it is impossible – and needless – to be totally comprehensive in any given reflection. We read in the Letter to the Hebrews that 'the word of God is something alive and active: it cuts like any double-edged sword, but more finely: it can slip through the place where the soul is divided from the spirit, or joints from the marrow; it can judge the secret emotions and thoughts' (Heb 4:12).

Hopefully, the reflections presented in this book will inspire readers to develop their own thoughts on, and responses to, the numerous practical lessons of the first readings in Year A. Written predominantly, but not solely, with a Catholic readership in mind, the book may also appeal to Christians from other traditions.

Earlier versions of some of the reflections were published in *The Catholic Times* and in the *Tipperary Star*.

LIST OF ABBREVIATIONS

(in alphabetical order of abbreviation)

Ac	Acts
1 Co	1 Corinthians
Dt	Deuteronomy
Ex	Exodus
Ezk	Ezekiel
Gn	Genesis
Heb	Hebrews
Ho	Hosea
Is	Isaiah
Jn	John
Jr	Jeremiah
1 K	1 Kings
2 K	2 Kings
Lk	Luke
Lv	Leviticus
Ml	Malachi
Mt	Matthew
Nb	Numbers
Pr	Proverbs
1 S	1 Samuel
Si	Ecclesiasticus (Sirach)
Ws	Wisdom
Zc	Zechariah
Zp	Zephaniah

REFLECTIONS

The Season of Advent

First Sunday of Advent

First reading: Is 2:1–5

Reflection

A new liturgical year begins as we celebrate the First Sunday of Advent and it is only proper that, in a truly joyous liturgical spirit, we wish one another a Happy New Year! The church's year does not coincide with the calendar year. Nevertheless, it is appropriate that, during these first days of the Advent season, we make some New Year's resolutions about improving our spiritual lives, just as we often make resolutions about changing other aspects of our lives at the end of every December while awaiting the beginning of January.

Advent, which in the Christian context means waiting for the arrival of the Messiah, is about new beginnings: the beginning of a new liturgical year, the beginning of our annual commemoration of the fulfilment of God's promise to send the Messiah at the first Christmas, the beginning of our yearly focus on preparing for the Second Coming of Jesus Christ.

New beginnings usually bring new opportunities and renewed enthusiasm. And Advent is no different. The next few weeks will provide us with the possibility of rekindling our hope in God's saving love and of rediscovering the Christian vision for a new earth when the Lord comes again at the end of time.

Such a vision is depicted in the first part (chapters 1–39) of the Book of Isaiah, who is one of the great Advent people in the Bible. Isaiah was the son of Amoz and a prophet living during the eighth century before the coming of Christ. He described his vision of the final emergence of the kingdom of God on this earth. In this vision of the future, Isaiah saw people walking in the Lord's paths instead of being enslaved to their sinful lives.

According to Isaiah's vision, people 'will hammer their swords into ploughshares, their spears into sickles' (Is 2:4). In addition, nations will no longer 'lift sword' against other nations and 'there will be no more training for war' (Is 2:4). There will be great prosperity and happiness when the peoples of this world eventually live in harmony and humbly turn towards God. Thus Isaiah offered his listeners the hope of a better future that God has predestined for everyone.

Sadly, there is terrible violence and much unnecessary hardship in the war-stricken world of today, where countless numbers of innocent people are being killed or displaced. It seems that they have no chance of a safe and happy future. There is hopelessness all around us. Therefore, we never needed Isaiah's message of hope so much. Likewise, we never needed to be challenged more by the implications of his message.

Isaiah's vision will not be fulfilled until human beings realise that peace on earth cannot happen without God. Throughout thousands of years of sinful living, human beings have frequently abandoned God and damaged severely the peace and justice of God's creation. This integrity can only be restored by God, and we are invited by God to become partners who contribute to the restoration of creation by being committed to the teaching of Christ and his church. Faithfulness to this teaching in our daily lives will ensure that we will indeed experience Isaiah's vision of a new earth when the Lord returns.

During Advent, we are encouraged to renew our commitment to being partners with God and disciples of Jesus. We await Jesus' coming among us (both at Christmas and at the end of time) in joyful hope. Meanwhile, we resolve to change our sinful lives so that we will be ready to welcome him.

What are some New Year's resolutions that we can make spiritually for this new church year? How can we contribute to making our world more peaceful and just when so many others are causing death and destruction? In what ways will we be more faithful to the teaching of Christ and his church by the end of this Advent? Now is the time to begin anew.

For meditation

Come, let us go up to the mountain of YHWH, to the Temple of the God of Jacob that he may teach us his ways so that we may walk in his paths. (Is 2:3)

Prayer

Father in heaven,
our hearts desire the warmth of your love
and our minds are searching for the light of your Word.
Increase our longing for Christ our Saviour

and give us the strength to grow in love,
that the dawn of his coming
may find us rejoicing in his presence
and welcoming the light of his truth.
We ask this in the name of Jesus the Lord.

Second Sunday of Advent

First reading: Is 11:1–10

Reflection
When the prophet Isaiah described the future Messiah (the Anointed One, the Saviour) he said that integrity would be 'the loincloth round his waist' and faithfulness would be 'the belt about his hips' (Is 11:5). As we journey through Advent each one of us may well ask metaphorically: What do we identify as the loincloth round our waist and the belt about our hips? Our prayerful wish can surely be that they are integrity and faithfulness.

Advent is not only about the beginning of a new church year. It is also about a new beginning for us because, once again, we resolve to live the Christian life sincerely while we wait for the Messiah's arrival. Integrity and faithfulness to the truth are essential traits of Christian living. Without them we can neither recognise the Messiah nor be credible witnesses to him.

Isaiah and the other Old Testament prophets prepared the people of Israel for the Messiah's coming. They reminded the people that God was always faithful and would never abandon them. Similarly, Advent teaches us that God's love is unfailing and it helps us to be ready for the Messiah in our own lives. We are encouraged to acknowledge that God is indeed our Saviour.

According to Isaiah, the Messiah would spring 'from the stock of Jesse' (Is 11:1). In other words, the Messiah would undo the effects of the sinful practices that had destroyed the people's integrity. When the Messiah would come, the unimaginable would happen. He would bring liberation to those who were poor and oppressed, especially in the spiritual sense. Life would never be the same again for anyone.

Thus, as we read Isaiah's prophecies during these early days of Advent, we are filled with hope. We are invited to rejoice that God will work many wonders through the Messiah in our lives and in the world.

When the Messiah returns, he will herald a new era of peace throughout the world. There will no longer be enmity between nations and human beings will live harmoniously with nature. Amazingly, the infant will play 'over the cobra's hole' in an ideal world, and the young child will safely put a hand 'into the viper's lair' (Is 11:8). This seems incredible and impossible. But nothing is impossible for God, and the unimaginable will happen. What is now considered the norm will be turned on its head.

However, we cannot become complacent because there was also a serious warning in Isaiah's message. He criticised severely the moral shortcomings of the people and he told them that external sacrifices were meaningless unless accompanied by interior conversion. He told them that they would be punished for their sins because the Messiah would deliver justice to those who had exploited other people. Therefore, Isaiah challenged his listeners to repent and change their lifestyles.

He does the same to us. During Advent we rejoice that the Messiah has already come and we prepare to welcome him again whenever he returns. But we also undergo conversion so that integrity and faithfulness to the truth will become the loincloths around our waists and the belt about our hips again. We pray that, like the Messiah, we will be full of God's spirit: 'a spirit of wisdom and insight, a spirit of counsel and power, a spirit of knowledge and of the fear of YHWH' (Is 11:2).

For meditation

He does not judge by appearances, he gives no verdict on hearsay, but judges the wretched with integrity, and with equity gives a verdict for the poor of the land. (Is 11:3–4)

Prayer

Father in heaven,
the day draws near when the glory of your Son

will make radiant the night of the waiting world.
May the lure of greed not impede us from the joy
which moves the hearts of those who seek him.
May the darkness not blind us
to the vision of wisdom
which fills the minds of those who find him.
We ask this in the name of Jesus the Lord.

Third Sunday of Advent

First reading: Is 35:1–6, 10

Reflection
The prophet Isaiah preached what seemed to be an unbelievable message. The wilderness would cease to be barren and would become fertile. The drylands would 'exult'. The wasteland would 'rejoice and bloom' (Is 35:1). In short, there would be no more sorrow and lament.

But how could all this happen? Isaiah was unequivocal. God was coming and nothing was impossible for God because he was the Creator and Lord of the heavens and the earth. There was every reason for the people to rejoice and be glad.

Thus Isaiah shared a message of great hope with God's people. He told them that God was coming and that life would never be the same again. The world would be utterly transformed with the arrival of the kingdom of God and a new era of peace and unity would be inaugurated. Isaiah's message was especially relevant for the people at that time because their morale was low and they were despairing.

Isaiah used particularly evocative imagery to communicate his message of hope. For example, he spoke about the wilderness, which was very familiar to the people. They had often been lost in the wilderness, surrounded by desolation, wandering aimlessly and unable to escape to a better life. In the wilderness, they had to struggle in order to survive and their daily lives were fraught with all kinds of danger. Just as the physical wilderness was not a happy place, the spiritual drought suffered by the people as they came to a realisation of the consequences of having abandoned God was a source of great pain for them.

Advent is about waiting for God to come. The unfolding Advent story symbolises our personal journeying out of the wilderness of sin, where we have become spiritual slaves, to the Promised Land of reconciliation, where we are happy in God's abiding presence. Whenever sin, especially serious sin, is a reality in our lives, we remain surrounded by the damage caused by it. We also continue to drift aimlessly through life without any meaningful sense of purpose. We are certainly not preparing to meet the Lord when he comes, either at Christmas or at the end of our lives.

Just as Isaiah prophesied to the Chosen People that the desolate wilderness would be transformed into luxuriant vegetation, a new and beautiful creation, Advent provides us with an opportunity to move from spiritual death to life in all its fullness. Advent is about the partnership between God and us. It is about the generosity of God's call and our wholehearted response to that call. God continually assures us that, in responding, we do not have to journey through the wilderness alone because he is accompanying us.

God never leaves us unprotected. But we need to learn to have courage. It is possible with God's help to move from the hopelessness of sin to the hope of everlasting joy and fulfilment. We are indeed capable of discovering hope in the midst of hopelessness. Like the Chosen People, we do not have to stay in the wilderness indefinitely.

Of course, the wilderness does not have to be interpreted totally in a totally negative sense. We read in the Bible that the prophets, including John the Baptist and Jesus, went into the wilderness, where they were freed from distractions, to focus on the word of God and to prepare for their public ministries.

In terms of the wilderness being a metaphor for our alienation from God because of sin, however, we might well ask the following questions: do we experience a sense of the wilderness in our lives now and, if we do, how do we understand it and relate to it? Are there any sinful patterns in our behaviour that are enslaving us? How might we be completely transformed by

God's grace into a new and beautiful creation? Let us use these Advent weeks to renew our responses to God's call so that we will be ready to meet the Lord when he comes.

For meditation
Then the eyes of the blind shall be opened, the ears of the deaf unsealed, then the lame shall leap like a deer and the tongues of the dumb sing for joy. (Is 35:5–6)

Prayer
Father of our Lord Jesus Christ,
ever faithful to your promises
and ever close to your church:
the earth rejoices in hope of the Saviour's coming
and looks forward with longing
to his return at the end of time.
Prepare our hearts and remove the sadness
that hinders us from feeling the joy and hope
which his presence will bestow,
for he is Lord for ever and ever.

Fourth Sunday of Advent

First reading: Is 7:10–14

Reflection
The Bible is the inspired word of God and, being Christians, we believe that the Old Testament foreshadowed (that is, not just predated but informed and was fulfilled in) the New Testament. This means that God's promise to be faithful to the covenant that he made with the Chosen People in the Old Testament was realised in the fullest sense with the birth of Jesus in the New Testament.

Approaching the end of Advent, we might recall that eight centuries before the birth of Jesus, the prophet Isaiah encouraged King Ahaz to trust, God who would protect the kingdom of Judah from the military threats of the neighbouring nations. He advised Ahaz to ask God for a 'sign' (Is 7:14) of this protection. Isaiah knew that God, rather than any military alliance or surrender, was the nation's best hope. But Ahaz refused to ask because, not trusting God, he had already decided to surrender to the Assyrians and did not want to change his plan.

Isaiah insisted on giving Ahaz a sign from God anyway: 'the maiden is with child and will soon give birth to a son whom she will call Immanuel' (Is 7:14).

This foreshadowing of the Virgin Birth is one of the doctrines that we ponder during the time of waiting for the coming of the Messiah. We are now in the final days of Advent, and Christmas is almost here. Our waiting will end shortly when we commemorate the birth of Jesus. His birth was the culmination of God's involvement with human beings over many centuries because, as the Bible teaches, Jesus was (and, of course, still is) the Messiah who, as God promised, would save and rule the world.

Moreover, the traditional Christian interpretation of Isaiah's prophecy, beginning with Matthew's Gospel (1:22–3), is that it refers to Jesus who was born of the Virgin Mary. He is the long-awaited Immanuel, he is God-with-us. From the beginning, God has always loved his people, and Jesus is the perfect expression of God's love because he is the Word made flesh (God-become-human).

The name Immanuel clearly describes Jesus' unique identity. He is truly God-with-us because he is both divine and human. This means that the Son of God is identical with the historical Jesus of Nazareth who was born in Bethlehem. God has never been remote from this world, although people have sometimes thought so – and some people still think like that. The real explanation is that we often abandon God. God does not force himself on anyone, but the fact that he made an irrevocable commitment to the human race by sending his Son into the world is the ultimate proof that God never abandons us.

God lived among his Chosen People while they journeyed through the wilderness for forty years on their journey to the Promised Land. So, too, God is present with us now while we spend our earthly lives preparing for eternal life. God could not give us a more convincing sign than Jesus, whose Real Presence is found in the Eucharist, that he is active in our world and in our lives.

The twin themes of promise and fulfilment are central to Advent. Approaching the end of Advent, then, we prepare to celebrate the fulfilment of God's promise to send the Messiah. We pray that, unlike Ahaz, we will listen to the various prophetic voices assuring us of God's loving presence and challenging us to trust God. We also pray that we will always believe that Jesus is both divine and human. As we complete our last-minute preparations for Christmas, let us not forget its real message: God-is-with-us.

For meditation
The maiden is with child and will soon give birth to a son. (Is 7:14)

Prayer
Father, all-powerful God,
your Eternal Word took flesh on our earth
when the Virgin Mary placed her life
at the service of your plan.
Lift our minds in watchful hope
to hear the voice which announces his glory
and open our minds to receive the Spirit
who prepares us for his coming.
We ask this through Christ our Lord.

The Season of Christmas

The Nativity of the Lord

First reading (Vigil Mass): Is 62:1–5
First reading (Midnight Mass): Is 9:1–7
First reading (Dawn Mass): Is 62:11–12
First reading (Mass during the Day): Is 52:7–10

Reflection
One of the most memorable scenes from the acclaimed 1980 movie, *Brubaker* (starring Robert Redford), was when Henry Brubaker – who had entered Wakefield prison farm disguised as an inmate so that he could experience directly the levels of corruption, abuse and violence that were endemic there – disclosed that he was the newly appointed warden. It happened when he identified himself during a particularly tense standoff, to the utter amazement of prisoners and prison officers alike, and ordered the immediate release of several prisoners who had been locked away in the dark for long periods of time.

On coming into the daylight, these convicts were literally blinded by the brightness around them. So Brubaker provided them with sunglasses to help their sensitive eyes to adjust gradually to their dramatically changed environment. After that incident, the movie recounts how Brubaker attempted to reform the unjust and oppressive prison regime by implementing his admirable ideals of truth and justice.

He achieved important success in some areas but, ultimately, he was rejected by the state governor and officials who deemed his term of office to be a failure. However, as he departed the prison, his efforts at reform were openly acknowledged by the many inmates and some prison staff who had benefited from the huge difference he had made to their lives.

The image of the unexpected release of those unfortunate prisoners from the darkness into the bright sunshine, and their initial inability to cope, helps us to appreciate the significance of the words spoken by the prophet Isaiah: 'The people that walked in darkness has seen a great light; on those who live in a land of deep shadow a light has shone' (Is 9:1).

This is the almost incredible message of Christmas: what happened then, with the birth of the Light of the World, puts the experience of the prisoners in *Brubaker* coming out of a long period of physical darkness 'in the shade', so to speak.

Our Saviour is already in our midst but we do not always recognise his presence. It often takes some dramatic intervention by God, which had been foretold by the prophets, for us to realise that we have been blessed by the loving presence of Jesus. The brightness of his light shines on us, dispelling the darkness of the sin that has imprisoned us and curtailed our freedom.

While Isaiah's use of the terms 'yoke', 'bar' and 'rod' (Is 9:3) was a reflection on the fact that King Ahaz's wife – who was barren – had given birth to a son named Hezekiah, later Christian commentators interpreted these terms as bringing hope and peace because the burdens of oppression and enslavement to sin were removed by the Saviour whom they understood to be 'Wonder-Counsellor, Mighty-God, Eternal-Father, Prince-of-Peace' (Is 9:5). The birth of Christ, which we commemorate and celebrate today, is the fulfilment of Isaiah's prophecy. His coming into our world has changed human life and history forever because he has lifted the burden of sin by bringing deliverance – if only we will accept it.

Christmas is a clear statement that our time of wandering in the dark is ended. Our lives and world now radiate the presence of the Prince of Peace, Jesus Christ our Lord and Saviour. It is only natural to say, then, that we rejoice and are glad. We do so not merely because God became human and lived among us, but because he has remained among us in his church, which speaks with the voice of his authority and through the life-giving power of his sacraments. This is truly a cause for rejoicing.

For meditation
For there is a child born for us, a son given to us and dominion is laid on his shoulders. (Is 9:5–6)

Prayer
Lord our God,
with the birth of your Son,
your glory breaks on the world.
Through the night hours of the darkened earth
we your people watch for the coming of your promised Son.
As we wait, give us a foretaste of the joy that you will grant us

when the fullness of his glory has filled the earth,
who lives and reigns with you for ever and ever.

The Holy Family of Jesus, Mary and Joseph

First reading: Si 3:2–6, 12–14

Reflection
How do we honour our fathers and mothers? For instance, if they are dead, in what ways do we value our memories of them and do we pray for them? Initially, we may think that these questions, especially the first, are specifically asked of children and teenagers. But they are addressed to all of us, regardless of our age or status. All adults, many of whom are parents, are also children and, consequently, are regularly challenged by the word of God to honour their own parents.

The command to honour our parents requires much more than respect. We are required to respect everyone because they have been created by God. But to honour means more than respect. It equates with cherishing. Whenever we cherish people, we consider them invaluable.

Obedience is a duty to our parents. The Fourth Commandment demands it. However, obedience needs to be interpreted more broadly than merely doing what we are told to do. While that is important, obedience also includes being reverent and supportive because it implies that we listen actively, with the intention of responding respectfully. Obedience also means being loyal and sincere towards our parents. And it means having a caring attitude towards them.

Our parents rightfully deserve our attention, affection and concern. When they become elderly, they ought to be enabled to enjoy a comfortable and peaceful retirement. We cannot ignore them if they are infirm and we can never justify treating them in such a way that they feel useless, redundant and irrelevant. It is saddening to visit elderly people in nursing homes and discover that some of them are rarely, if ever, visited by their adult children. Such situations suggest that, in many instances, elderly parents are dishonoured and mistreated.

In a society where there is so much emphasis on youthfulness and invincibility, the elderly are frequently forgotten. They are sometimes judged to be a burden. Yet we forget that, during their younger years, most parents made significant personal sacrifices so that they could provide for their children. Just as children are our link with hopes and dreams for the future, the elderly are our link with the traditions and heritage of the past.

At the most basic level, common courtesy and decency teach us that one good turn deserves another. Thus it is only right and just that we care for our parents and other elderly relatives so that we can return some of their kindness and love. In addition, our Christian faith challenges us to honour and care for the elderly.

We need to remember that older people have accumulated much wisdom and experience during their lives. If we appreciate them and are prepared to learn from them, they can save us much hardship and inconvenience because they teach us not to make the same mistakes that they made. They usually have many values and lessons about everyday living to share with us.

Christmas is a time for families. It provides an opportunity to visit our parents and other elderly people and to let them know that we love them and that they matter to us. Interestingly, children and grandparents have an especially strong relationship. Children are instinctively attracted to their grandparents, seemingly aware of the richness of life-experience that comes with older age. They love to listen to their grandparents' stories about when they were young. Significantly, grandparents and other elderly relatives often make the most important contributions to the faith development of children.

The Feast of the Holy Family invites us to renew our commitment to family life. We thank God for everyone in our families and we offer our love and affection to aging parents as a sign that we cherish them and are grateful for the life they shared with us and the sacrifices they made while rearing us.

For meditation

Long life comes to him who honours his father, he who sets his mother at ease is showing obedience to the Lord. (Si 3:6–7)

Prayer
Father in heaven, Creator of all,
you ordered the earth to bring forth life
and crowned its goodness by creating the family of humankind.
In history's moment when all was ready,
you sent your Son to dwell in time,
obedient to the laws of life in our world.
Teach us the sanctity of human love,
show us the value of family life,
and help us to live in peace with all human beings
that we may share in your life for ever.
We ask this through Christ our Lord.

Solemnity of Mary, Mother of God

First reading: Nb 6:22–7

Reflection
Many of us are familiar with the well-known Irish ballad with the lines: 'A mother's love is a blessing, no matter where you roam … Love her as in childhood.' This song undoubtedly acknowledges the value of motherhood because it communicates unmistakably that a mother's love is indeed a blessing.

Fortunately, most people have a wonderful relationship with their mother. When a mother is at her best, she praises and encourages her children – and even scolds them if necessary in their best interest – regardless of their age or status in society. Mothers simply never cease being mothers. They never stop seeing us as their children because they always want what is best for us. As little children we constantly seek our mother's affirmation and approval. In this way, our mother makes a major contribution to the development of our self-esteem.

Today we celebrate the Solemnity of Mary, the Mother of God. In much the same way as we appreciate our earthly mother's love as a genuine and welcome blessing, we know that Mary's blessing as our spiritual mother is also to be greatly valued and cherished. Her love for us grows out of God's love for her and his sharing of his life with her in a truly special manner. She learned how to love with all her heart through loving and following her Son, Jesus, throughout his ministry – and by constantly pondering his teaching and example – and we are the beneficiaries of that love as it blesses us in our relationships and activities.

God chose to send the Saviour to us only when Mary had given her fiat, her 'yes', thus revealing the pivotal role that she played in salvation history. God could have sent his Son on earth in any number of ways. That he chose to do so through Mary is of huge significance: God chose to give us both the Saviour and a heavenly mother. God does nothing without good reason. So it is good to reflect on this truth whenever we reflect on Mary's love for us.

In developing our relationship with Our Lady, we are well advised to practise what is recommended in the old Irish ballad. In other words, by applying the message to Our Lady, we learn the value of loving her as we did in childhood. This is very important because that is how we remain close to our earthly mother. Children love their mothers with a remarkable innocence and trust. It is only as they get older that they often forget about the singularly important role their mothers have played in their lives.

We all know that a mother who sincerely loves her children would do anything for them, even to the point of laying down her life for them. She would do without the necessities of life herself so that her children would have what they need to survive and mature as human beings. That is what Mary, the Mother of God, and our spiritual mother, is willing to do for us. She intercedes for us. She watches over us. She teaches and encourages us. She obtains God's grace for us in our attempts to live according to the teaching of Christ and his church.

In the Book of Numbers, we read that God told Moses to say to Aaron and his descendents: 'May YHWH bless you and keep you. May YHWH let his face shine on you and be gracious to you. May YHWH uncover his face to you and bring you peace' (Nb 6:24–6). We can be certain that God tells Mary to say the same to us – and much more. In conveying God's blessing to us, Mary is also conveying her own blessing because her blessing of us originates in God's blessing of her. Is it any wonder, then, that a mother's love is a blessing, no matter where we roam?

For meditation
May YHWH bless you and keep you. May YHWH let his face shine on you and be gracious to you. May YHWH uncover his face to you and bring you peace. (Nb 6:24–6)

Prayer
Father,
source of life in every age,
the Virgin conceived and bore your Son
who is called Wonderful God, Prince of peace.
May her prayer, the gift of a mother's love,
be your people's joy through all ages.
May her response, born of a humble heart,
draw your Spirit to rest on your people.
Grant this through Christ our Lord.

Second Sunday after Christmas

First reading: Si 24:1–2, 8–12

Reflection
We sometimes hear criticisms of the Christian claim that the Old Testament anticipates the New Testament. Some people struggle with the Christian belief that the Hebrew scriptures implicitly convey many hints about the future Messiah which, when combined with the more explicit information in the New Testament, provide the basis for the articulation of the church's doctrines about Jesus Christ, whose birth we commemorate and joyfully celebrate at Christmas. This may seem incredible chronologically, but we know that both the Old and New Testaments contain the inspired word of God.

The Book of Sirach (also known as the Book of Ecclesiasticus) personifies an attribute of God that is very relevant during the Christmas season. It refers to the Wisdom of God (expressed in feminine terms) which, in the New Testament and especially in John's Gospel, is further developed and understood as the Word (as distinct from word) of God. Christmas celebrates the truth that 'the Word was made flesh' and that 'he lived among us' (Jn 1:14). This means that God became a human being in Jesus, that the Creator became a creature. Jesus is the Eternal Word.

In Ecclesiasticus, Wisdom tells us: 'Then the creator of all things instructed me, and he who created me fixed a place for my tent. He said, "Pitch your tent in Jacob, make Israel your inheritance." From eternity, in the beginning, he created me, and for eternity I shall remain' (Si 24:8–9). Thus the biblical text began to hint at the Incarnation long before it really happened.

Significantly, Wisdom pre-existed the creation of the earth and was present with God when creation occurred. More significantly, according to Sirach, Wisdom has 'taken root in a privileged people in the Lord's property, in his inheritance' (Si 24:12). Essentially, the Wisdom of God has pitched her tent among the Chosen People.

This foreshadows the New Testament reference to the Word becoming flesh and living among us – the Word that, in the beginning, was with God and was God. Thus the Wisdom of God in the Old Testament and the Word of God in the New Testament are aspects of God's nature and self-communication.

Christmas celebrates the birth of the infant Jesus, which is, understandably, a story of great human interest. But it also celebrates the Word becoming flesh, which is a most sublime mystery that is beyond human comprehension. Therefore, the human authors of the Bible needed to use the language of symbol, metaphor and personification in addition to ordinary, everyday language, in trying to express adequately what actually happened at Christmas. Otherwise, they would not have been able to explore and present any meaningful sense of the absolute Mystery of God. The biblical concept of Wisdom offers us an insight into the unfolding Christmas story from God's perspective instead of from our perspective.

At Christmas we celebrate the threefold birth of Jesus, the Son of God. He is born in the mind and heart of God the Father. He is born from the womb of the Virgin Mary, and he is born anew in the heart of the believer. How has he been born anew in our hearts this year? In what ways do we respond with joy and gratitude for the inspiration of the Wisdom of God and the reality of the Word of God becoming flesh?

On this day, let us remind ourselves what Saint Paul of the Cross (1694–1775) taught: 'Celebrate the feast of Christmas every day, even every moment in the interior temple of your spirit, remaining like a baby in the bosom of the heavenly Father, where you will be reborn each moment in the Divine Word, Jesus Christ.'

For meditation
I have taken root in a privileged people in the Lord's property, in his inheritance. (Si 24:12)

Prayer
Father of our Lord Jesus Christ,
our glory is to stand before the world
as your own sons and daughters.
May the simple beauty of Jesus' birth
summon us always to love what is most deeply human,
and to see your Word made flesh
reflected in those whose lives we touch.
We ask this through Christ our Lord.

The Epiphany of the Lord

First reading: Is 60:1–6

Reflection
In his homily for the Feast of the Epiphany in 2011, Pope Benedict XVI said:

> [An] important element of the event of the Magi appears to us very clearly: the language of creation enables us to

make good headway on the path towards God but does not give us the definitive light. In the end, it was indispensable for the Magi to listen to the voice of the sacred scriptures: they alone could show them the way. The true star is the word of God which, amidst the uncertainty of human discourses, gives us the immense splendour of the Divine Truth.

For many of us, today's feast heralds the end of the Christmas season. Yet the Epiphany cannot be separated from the heart of the Christmas message. The word 'epiphany' means 'manifestation' or 'showing'. Fundamentally, the Christian vocation is to show Jesus and his glory to the world. The Epiphany acknowledges that Jesus Christ, the newborn baby, is the Saviour of all people. Salvation has come and is for everyone, if they will accept it and reform their lives accordingly, not only the few.

During the days of Christmas, we reflect on what it means to believe that the Word became flesh (God became human) and lived among us. God has chosen to live among us, his people, in the person of Jesus Christ, our Lord and Saviour, who saves us from the justly deserved consequences of our sins.

This is why we enter into the spirit and meaning of Christmas. All other activities associated with Christmas – for example, the exchange of gifts, the holidays from school and work, the visits to family and friends – are secondary. The real wonder of Christmas is not just that God became human in and through his Son, Jesus Christ, but that Christ, through his church, continues to be present in our world. Knowing and experiencing this truth brings us consolation, hope and confidence, in the same way as the people living in exile during the time of Isaiah were encouraged by his preaching. Isaiah's prophetic sayings were fulfilled in Christ.

Christmas and the Epiphany challenge us to renew our appreciation of the commitment God has made to us by becoming a human being like us in all things except sin. In the person and life of Jesus Christ, the Word made flesh, God has demonstrated beyond all doubt how much he loves us and desires to share his life with us. God shares his life with us especially through the church and the celebration of the sacraments. In the person and life of Jesus Christ, God has embraced human nature completely and he has become one with it. This is the mystery of Christmas and it remains true for all time and for all God's people everywhere.

Therefore, we can ask: how would we respond to God's spokesperson saying to us 'Arise, shine out, for your light has come, the glory of the Lord is rising on you' (Is 60:1)? Imagine hearing those words during a time of economic recession and increasing hopelessness – such as the present. If the person speaking to us was genuine, credible and truly prophetic, we would surely be impressed and we might even begin to think that divine providence was going to bring real hope in a seemingly hopeless situation. This is the significance of celebrating the Epiphany.

The Epiphany invites us to consider once again the fuller meaning of Christmas and to respond accordingly. The wise men, in presenting Jesus with gifts of gold, frankincense and myrrh, acknowledged him as Saviour of all people. The feast invites us to ask: what gifts can we present to Jesus that acknowledge him as our Saviour?

Surely one of the most appropriate gifts we can offer to Our Lord is striving to live a life that imitates his teaching and example. Therefore, this is an ideal time to reflect on the practice of our Christian faith so that, during the coming year, we will 'show' the world the glory of the Saviour who has redeemed us from sin and who gives us life through the sacramental life of the church.

In that 2011 Epiphany homily, Pope Benedict also said:

> Let us allow ourselves to be guided by the star that is the word of God, let us follow it in our lives, walking with the church in which the Word has pitched his tent. Our road will always be illumined by a light that no other sign can give us. And we too shall become stars for others, a reflection of that light which Christ caused to shine upon us.

For meditation
Arise, shine out [Jerusalem], for your light has come, the glory of YHWH is rising on you, though night still covers the earth and darkness the peoples. (Is 60:1–2)

Prayer
Father of light, unchanging God,
today you reveal to people of faith
the resplendent fact of the Word made flesh.
Your light is strong,
your love is near;
draw us beyond the limits which this world imposes,
to the life where your Spirit makes all life complete.
We ask this through Christ our Lord.

The Baptism of the Lord

First reading: Is 42: 1–4, 6–7

Reflection
Traditionally, Christians have believed that the suffering servant in the Book of Isaiah is a metaphor for the promised Messiah, Jesus the Christ, who would come into the world sometime in the future to secure salvation for those who would decide to turn away from the deadly consequences of sin. The New Testament writings and the Tradition of the church support this understanding.

According to the prophet Isaiah, the servant would be specially chosen by God and would be consecrated to God. He would be holy, kind, compassionate and faithful. Alas, he would suffer while inaugurating a new era of justice and peace on earth – a peace that the world itself would be unable to give.

Hence the title: suffering servant. The Christ who was to come would take upon himself the sins and transgressions of all people. He would experience hostility because his efforts to convince people about God's love and his challenge to be faithful to God's commandments would be despised by many and would make him unpopular.

Ironically, as people would reject the suffering servant, he would heal their spiritual blindness and liberate them from their enslavement to sin. He would be a light to all the world's nations, showing them God's mercy. In doing what God had asked him to do, he would make a meaningful difference in people's lives. Not surprisingly, the suffering servant would be a humble servant in whom God would delight.

Christmas celebrated the fulfilment of Isaiah's prophecy as we commemorated the birth of Jesus in Bethlehem, the first coming of the Saviour into human history. In the Incarnation, the all-powerful God made himself a humble servant to respond to the spiritual needs of human beings.

Later, when Jesus was baptised at the beginning of his public ministry, Isaiah's prophecy was realised again as God reaffirmed his choice of Jesus as the Messiah. Jesus was the Suffering Servant who, through his obedience and perseverance, delighted God. But, significantly, Jesus' baptism was not only about God's choice of him, it was also about Jesus' response in faith.

Similarly, our baptism did not only mark God's choice of us. It also marked our response to God. At baptism, we were invited to imitate the example of Jesus the Suffering Servant. We were called to be holy, merciful and faithful. We were challenged to work for truth and justice – knowing that, wherever truth and love are found, justice flourishes.

The Suffering Servant brought salvation to the world. When we were baptised we were asked to share the saving message of God's love and to bring healing and God's grace to those around us. In summary, we were commissioned to be servants in whom God delights.

As we celebrate the Feast of the Baptism of Jesus, we pray that we will be faithful to our baptismal commitment. This means that we strive to be holy as God is holy and that we work diligently to rid our lives of sin. There can be no room for sin in our lives if we are serious about our baptism. We are indeed chosen by God. However, with that choice is a necessary response. How do we understand and describe our response to being baptised? How might other people observe us to be humble servants in whom

God delights because we are faithful to the great commandment to love God and our neighbour?

For meditation
Here is my servant whom I uphold, my chosen one in whom my soul delights. (Is 42:1)

Prayer
Father in heaven,
you revealed Christ as your Son
by the voice that spoke over the waters of the Jordan.
May all who share in the sonship of Christ
follow in his path of service to humankind,
and reflect the glory of his kingdom
even to the ends of the earth,
for he is Lord for ever and ever.

The Season of Lent

First Sunday of Lent

First reading: Gn 2:7–9; 3:1–7

Reflection
During Lent, when we prepare to commemorate the death and resurrection of Christ, and celebrate the newness of life he shares with us at Easter, we are challenged to evaluate our lives in the context of our Christian faith and the teaching of Christ and his church. Also, we are encouraged to repent of our sins and to do penance for them so that we can renew and deepen our relationship with Christ. That is why Lent is characterised by prayer, fasting and almsgiving.

At the beginning of Lent we read extracts from the Book of Genesis. Genesis teaches us much that is relevant to our daily lives. The first lesson is that God has created us out of 'dust from the soil'. We are living beings only because God 'breathed a breath of life' (Gn 2:7) into us. This implies that we are nothing without God. We could not even exist were it not for God's creative and life-sharing love.

Sometimes we deny this fundamental truth about ourselves and we forget that all we are and have comes from God. That is why the priest may remind us on Ash Wednesday, as he places ashes on our foreheads: 'Remember you are dust and to dust you will return.'

The Genesis story also teaches us about the origins of sin in human nature. Sin is essentially injurious and detrimental to our relationship with God. It occurs when, because of our decisions to disregard God's will, we alienate ourselves from God.

Adam and Eve experienced this after yielding to the serpent's temptation. Their sin resulted not only from external temptation but also from their inner-pride. Although God had given them the marvellous gift of free will, they were unwilling to accept the limitation that God had put on it. They became victims of their innate tendency towards self-centredness.

In Genesis we read that, before they sinned, Adam and Eve walked happily around God's garden enjoying its beauty and food. They had a harmonious relationship with God. All was well. However, after they had eaten fruit from the forbidden tree, 'the eyes of both of them were opened and they realised that they were naked' (Gn 3:7).

This contrasted significantly with what the serpent had told them earlier: 'on the day you eat [the fruit] your eyes will be opened and you will be like gods, knowing good and evil' (Gn 3:5). Their pride resulted in their estrangement from God and, immediately, they felt ashamed and guilty. Their sin was Original Sin, which had consequences for every other human being. It marked the beginning of the need for God's redemption so that human beings could have their intimate familiarity with God restored.

Ever since Original Sin, the most important task for human beings is to abandon sin and turn towards God asking for mercy. This is because sin damages and eventually destroys the integrity of our relationships with God and other people. That is why the priest may also remind us on Ash Wednesday to 'turn away from sin and be faithful to the gospel'.

At the root of every sin is human pride. We all have the tendency to put self-interest before the centrality of God in our lives and before the needs of others. Lent offers us an opportunity to surrender completely to God, recognising that without him we cannot exist because he is the giver of life. The discipline of Lenten penance, thereby making amends for our sins, helps us to appreciate our total dependence on God. Such conviction is the first step in our redemption from the consequences of our sins.

For meditation

YHWH God fashioned man of dust from the soil. Then he breathed into his nostrils a breath of life, and thus man became a living being. (Gn 2:7)

Prayer

Lord our God,
you formed human beings from the clay of the earth
and breathed into them the spirit of life,
but they turned from your face and sinned.
In this time of repentance
we call out for your mercy.
Bring us back to you

and to the life your Son won for us
by his death on the cross,
for he lives and reigns for ever and ever.

Second Sunday of Lent

First reading: Gn 12:1–4

Reflection
God's request of Abram was unusual. God promised him that he would become 'a great nation' (Gn 12:2) and that he would receive many blessings. Abram's name would become so famous that it would 'be used as a blessing' (Gn 12:2). Before all this would happen, however, God asked Abram to leave his country, his family and his home and travel to the land where God would lead him. Thus God's call to Abram invited a response, a response in faith.

One of the classic recurring themes in the Bible, fundamental to the spiritual life, is that of 'call and response'. God's call always invites a response. In doing so, God initiates and sustains a divine–human relationship that invites dialogue and a trusting partnership. Effectively, God begins the communication and awaits a response from us.

The most important attribute of this call-and-response theme is that it indicates a personal relationship between God and human beings, either individually or communally. God is personal and caring, wishing to be involved in human activities and history. Paradoxically, God – who is almighty and incomprehensible – is not distant and remote. Instead, God is nearby and intimately involved with us.

There is a significant difference between speaking and calling. To speak to someone does not necessitate that the person replies or responds. Speaking could, for example, involve the issuing of instructions or the passing of judgement, with no accompanying right of reply. However, to call someone implies that the person being called is asked to respond in some way, whether positively or negatively. Dialogue and engagement occur. People who call us are addressing us – because we are important to them. Their call often forms the basis of a relationship.

The unfolding biblical story of Abram (whose name subsequently changed to Abraham) is an account of his faithful response to God's call in circumstances that required tremendous courage and trust from Abram. The task God gave him required that he leave what was familiar to him and journey to an unknown destination with only God for his guide. Remarkably, Abram trusted God completely and began the journey immediately. The scriptures record that Abram indeed became the father of a great nation.

It is worth reflecting on the relationship between God and Abram because our relationships with God are intended to be similar. They are meant to be characterised by the call-and-response theme. We are challenged to trust God, who often calls us into an unknown future. We need to remember that with God on our side nobody can ultimately harm us.

As Christians, Jesus calls us to follow him every day. His call invites a response from us, as it did from the first disciples. Just as God assured Abram that he would offer guidance and protection, Jesus does the same for his disciples in and through his church. That is why we are called to be faithful to the church's teaching.

Regarding the call-and-response theme in our spirituality, Lent offers us a yearly opportunity to answer at least some of the following questions: what is our sense of being called by God and how does it compare with Abram's call? How could we respond authentically to God's call and how would our response manifest itself? If responding to God's call involves trust, are there different ways in which we can develop trusting relationships with God? How would we describe our commitment to the church's teaching?

God demanded much from Abram but the reward was great. God demands much of each one of us too and promises a great reward. How realistic is it for us to respond by letting go of our many comforts and securities and venturing out into the unknown, looking to the church for guidance and protection?

For meditation
Leave your country, your family and your father's house, for the land I will show you. (Gn 12:1)

Prayer
Father of light,
in you is found no shadow of change
but only the fullness of life and limitless truth.
Open our hearts to the voice of your Word
and free us from the original darkness that shadows our vision.
Restore our sight that we may look on your Son
who calls us to repentance and a change of heart,
for he lives and reigns with you for ever and ever.

Third Sunday of Lent

First reading: Ex 17:3–7

Reflection
How would we feel if we and our fellow citizens were described as a nation of complainers? I suspect that we would not be too pleased. None of us would freely admit that we were continually complaining about our various life situations. Yet this impression, which is often correct, is sometimes given about us and other people. It is as though we are invariably unhappy, despite the many blessings and graces we receive.

We read in the Old Testament that the Israelites were a nation of complainers while Moses was leading them through the wilderness to the Promised Land. They demonstrated their ingratitude to God whenever problems arose. They regularly blamed Moses for what they perceived as their misfortune and they challenged his leadership. In the Book of Exodus, we read that, on one occasion, 'tormented by thirst, the people complained against Moses. "Why did you bring us out of Egypt?" they said' (Ex 17:3). Furthermore, they doubted God by saying: 'Is YHWH with us, or not?' (Ex 17:7)

Although they were quick to complain, they were not so quick to begin working to alleviate their distress. Instead, they persistently moaned and groaned. They expected Moses and God to solve their problems by whatever means, even if the solutions required miracles.

Every time we read the biblical account of the Israelites wandering through the wilderness for forty years, we cannot but be astonished by God's faithfulness to them. Notwithstanding their ingratitude and lack of faith, God never abandoned them. His divine presence (*Shekinah*) was with them at all times and he provided for all their needs. If only they had believed this, they would have realised how futile it was to complain continually.

The people were concerned more about their immediate physical needs than about their long-term destiny. Their behaviour was influenced by their selfishness rather than by their gratitude to God for all he had done for them.

Moses's relationship with God was very different. That relationship was characterised by familiarity and intimacy, because Moses's faith taught him to trust God and his friendship with God matured because he freely responded in faith.

There is an important teaching here for us. As a people, we often behave like the Israelites in Moses's time. We quickly complain about the circumstances of our lives and we blame God and other people for many of our predicaments. We easily imitate the complaining crowds around us and we become moaners and groaners, waiting for someone else to solve our problems.

Constant moaning and groaning predispose us to wallowing in self-pity. Self-pity prevents us from trusting God and hinders us from doing anything to help ourselves. We need to remember that God helps those who help themselves. Nothing is impossible for God and he will never fail us. But we must learn to trust God in every situation. It is when God seems to be absent from our lives that he is most strongly present.

We recognise God's presence only in faith. But any true faith will die if we are always complaining. Lent offers us an opportunity, through the disciplines of praying, fasting and charitable works, to stop complaining about life and to put God and the needs of others before our own. Let us pray that our faith will be strengthened so that we will know that God is always with us and that there is much more to life than merely complaining.

For meditation
I shall be standing before you there on the rock, at Horeb. (Ex 17:6)

Prayer
God of all compassion, Father of all goodness,
to heal the wounds our sins and selfishness bring upon us
you bid us turn to fasting, prayer and sharing with our brothers and sisters.
We acknowledge our sinfulness, our guilt is ever before us:
when our weakness causes discouragement,
let your compassion fill us with hope
and lead us through a Lent of repentance to the beauty of Easter joy.
Grant this through Christ our Lord.

Fourth Sunday of Lent

First reading: 1 S 16:1, 6–7, 10–13

Reflection
We are easily reminded of the well-known fairy tale about Cinderella whenever we read the biblical account of God's choice of David to be the future king. Cinderella's two sisters and her stepmother were cruel to her and wrongly assumed that the prince, desperately searching for his mystery girl, could not possibly be interested in her because she was so unexciting and so ordinary. Unlike them, she stayed at home doing various tasks and chores while they were busy socialising and enjoying themselves. They are the example, par excellence, of selfishness at work in human beings.

According to these 'ugly sisters', there was nothing attractive about Cinderella. Nobody would want to know her or meet her.

She was unimportant. Yet we all know from listening to the fairy tale that the prince insisted on meeting Cinderella and, to the shock and dismay of her stepmother and sisters, he chose her to be his princess. Although to all intents and purposes she was rejected by her family, she was chosen by the prince. Then he married Cinderella and they lived happily ever after, in the way of all fairy tales.

Interestingly, there are some similarities between the Cinderella fairy tale and the biblical story about David. Like Cinderella, David was considered to be the least important member of his family. When Samuel arrived at Jesse's house, he was introduced to all Jesse's sons except David. David, the youngest son, remained outside looking after the sheep. Fortunately, Samuel insisted on meeting David and, when he met him, he knew immediately that David was God's chosen one. Although not invited to join his father and brothers, God chose David through Samuel. And Samuel anointed David as the future king of Israel.

An obvious message for us in this biblical story is that God's standards are quite different from our standards. God chooses the last instead of the first. God often surprises us because he does not discriminate between people based on age, looks and education. From the human perspective, we might easily think that God would have chosen one of Jesse's older, wiser and more capable sons. But God's ways are not our ways and the teaching of God's word challenges us to value and cherish all people because every human being has been created by God to know, love and serve him on this earth in preparation for eternal life with him in heaven.

In the twentieth century, God – through the Blessed Virgin Mary – chose three illiterate, peasant children in Fatima to remind us of the gospel's call to repentance. This proves again that God is more interested in what is in people's hearts than in their external appearances and status. We need to learn anew how to imitate God and the discipline of Lent helps us to do so.

Another important message from the David story relates to what happened to him after Samuel anointed him. We read that 'the spirit of YHWH seized on David and stayed with him from that day on' (1 S 16:13). This means that David was influenced and protected by the Holy Spirit. Each one of us has also been anointed, at baptism and again at confirmation. The Holy Spirit lives in us, prompting us to be faithful to the teaching of Christ and his church. We need to realise that we are temples of the Holy Spirit and live our lives accordingly.

King David, sadly, did not live happily ever after, unlike Cinderella. Regrettably, the king did not always respect the presence of the Holy Spirit in his life and he sinned seriously more than once. He often forgot that God had chosen him to be first rather than last among his family and people. However, God never abandoned him and called him to repentance. In the same way, God does not abandon us and we too are being invited to become repentant people during Lent.

For meditation
The spirit of YHWH seized on David and stayed with him from that day on.' (1 S 16:13)

Prayer
God our Father,
your Word, Jesus Christ, spoke peace to a sinful world
and brought humankind the gift of reconciliation
by the suffering and death he endured.
Teach us, the people who bear his name,
to follow the example he gave us:
may our faith, hope and charity
turn hatred to love, conflict to peace and death to eternal life.
We ask this through Christ our Lord.

Fifth Sunday of Lent

First reading: Ezk 37:12–14

Reflection
Sometimes we yearn for a new beginning or wish for another chance when life seems hopeless. Many people often think and

feel like that. Some of them are remorseful about broken relationships. Others have regrets about unpleasant happenings from long ago and they continue to live in the past, oblivious to all the blessings and opportunities in the present. Then there are those elderly parents, anxious about their children and grandchildren who always seem to be in trouble.

Unfortunately, modern life tends to be very stressful and, increasingly, some of us are unable to do much to alleviate our worry and despair. Unless we are striving to live truly Christian lives – spiritually, devotionally and morally – life often appears to be meaningless and we may feel powerless to change our particular circumstances.

During the lifetime of Ezekiel, one of the most important Old Testament prophets, the people of Israel were in exile from the Promised Land. They had been humiliated and they were downtrodden and discouraged. There did not seem to be any sign of a better future. The Israelites would have appreciated a new beginning, another chance. But how could that happen? In effect, their spirit was broken. As people often say, they might as well have been dead.

Amazingly, in the midst of their trials and tribulations, Ezekiel preached a message of hope to them. God, speaking through the prophet, assured them of a great future and called the Israelites to work towards that future. Life would improve for them again. They would return to Jerusalem and be recognised as God's Chosen People once more, although they needed to realise that they also had their own individual responsibilities.

We know from reading the Bible that God's word is powerful. It cannot fail. In the days of Ezekiel, we see evidence of the effectiveness of God's word, as revealed in sacred scripture: God's promises were – and are – always fulfilled and effective.

Ezekiel's preaching contains a crucial lesson for us. God's word is effective. God always speaks the truth and his word brings life, especially in difficult and hopeless situations. But we must learn to trust God's word. We need to believe God's promises, knowing that they will never be broken. All of these promises recorded in the Old Testament culminate in God's gift of Christ and the church to the world.

There is another lesson for us. God, speaking through Ezekiel, said to the Israelites: 'And I shall put my spirit in you, and you will live' (Ezk 37:14). God reassures us in the same way today when we are troubled and confused. He offers us life in abundance, primarily through the teaching of Christ and his church.

It is only by accepting individual responsibility for our actions that we can experience the same joyful new beginning that the ancient people of the Old Testament experienced after they had abandoned their infidelity to God and began a renewed friendship with him, having resolved to turn away from their sinful lifestyles. Whenever we are absolved from our sins in the sacrament of reconciliation, we enjoy a new beginning. There is no other new beginning to compare with this wonderful opportunity for a fresh spiritual start.

Lent is all about a new beginning, another chance. As we listen attentively to God's word, we learn that it is effective and we rediscover life's true meaning. In welcoming the hope and consolation offered by God's word, we recognise the challenge that it presents and the power that it gives us to change our lives through penance and charitable works as we prepare for Easter.

For meditation

I am now going to open your graves; I mean to raise you from your graves, my people, and lead you back to the soil of Israel. (Ezk 37:12)

Prayer

Father in heaven,
the love of your Son led him to accept the suffering of the cross
that his brothers and sisters might glory in new life.
Change our selfishness into self-giving.
Help us to embrace the world you have given us,
that we transform the darkness of its pain
into the life and joy of Easter.
Grant this through Christ our Lord.

Passion Sunday (Palm Sunday)

First reading: Is 50:4–7

Reflection
The famous saying of Edmund Burke (1729–97) that 'all that is necessary for the triumph of evil is that good [people] do nothing' is widely and frequently quoted by believers and non-believers alike. We live in a seriously troubled world where many people are confused and have lost their sense of purpose and meaning in life. Often what they really need is an encouraging word or a kind expression of concern. This would make such a difference to their well-being. It would renew their hope in the basic goodness of humanity.

Unfortunately, most of us are usually too busy to notice other people when they need a cheerful smile or a helping hand because, for at least some of us, life has become so self-centred that we are no longer interested in the welfare of others. Instead, we are constantly preoccupied with satisfying our own desires, indulging in our own perceived needs and wants.

But that is not what God intended. The truth is that we have been privileged and blessed by God in countless ways. Regardless of how difficult and demanding we may judge the particular circumstances of our own lives to be, there are always other people who, relatively speaking, are worse off than us. To help cope with the unfairness of life, we need to remember that God created human beings as social beings, desiring that we would cherish and support one another. Thus we need to live accordingly.

This applies as much to the spiritual well-being of others as it does to their physical and mental well-being. God commands us to love our neighbour as we love ourselves. This means that we humbly accept other people correcting our faults and failings. Similarly, we behave responsibly towards them by gently challenging them when they contravene God's commandments.

That is why, for example, the prophet Isaiah said: 'The Lord has given me a disciple's tongue. So that I may know how to reply to the wearied, he provides me with speech. Each morning he wakes me to hear, to listen like a disciple. The Lord has opened my ear' (Is 50:4–5).

What was true for Isaiah needs to be true for each one of us too. We are meant to speak encouraging words and to lend a helping hand to those around us who are less well off than ourselves, both materially and spiritually. We are obligated by our commitment to God's law to do so even to the extent of being prepared to lay down our lives for them or, more commonly, to risk unpopularity. God requires nothing more, nothing less. Every day God teaches us what we must do in order to please him in our work, leisure and dealings with others.

This is certainly a daunting challenge, but it is not impossible. We are never left alone, without God's loving presence and constant help, and God never asks us to do anything that is impossible. We need to remember scripture's often-repeated teaching that nothing is impossible for God. And we need to celebrate the church's sacraments regularly so that we can have the life of grace in our souls.

How are we using the gifts that God has given us, especially the gift of a disciple's tongue? What are the ways in which we offer encouragement to those who feel depressed and dejected? Are we able to speak the truth in every situation? God has opened our ears. So how do we listen? In what ways are we willing to change in response to what God is saying so that, in turn, we may empower others to grow in grace, thereby fulfilling God's will in their lives? Let us not forget that we are called to be saints.

For meditation

The Lord has given me a disciple's tongue. So that I may know how to reply to the wearied he provides me with speech. (Is 50:4)

Prayer

Almighty Father of our Lord Jesus Christ,
you sent your Son
to be born of woman and to die on a cross,
so that through the obedience of one man,
estrangement might be dissolved for all human beings.
Guide our minds by this truth
and strengthen our lives by the example of his death,
that we may live in union with you
in the kingdom of your promise.
Grant this through Christ our Lord.

The Season of Easter

Easter Sunday

Third Old Testament reading (Mass of Easter Night): Ex 14:15 – 15:1

First reading (Mass of the Day): Ac 10:34, 37–43

Reflection
At the Easter Vigil, the Liturgy of the Word contains seven readings from the Old Testament in addition to the two New Testament readings. (There are a total of nine readings.) These seven readings provide us with an overview of salvation history. Salvation history is the technical term used to explain how God has acted in creating the world and in gradually bringing it to fulfilment, after the first sin (known as Original Sin) committed by Adam and Eve, by sending the Messiah to free human beings from the consequences of their sins.

While all these readings are significant – if they were unimportant the church would not include them in the Vigil – the third reading (Ex 14:15 – 15:1) is particularly noteworthy. It describes the crossing of the Red Sea by the Israelites during their escape from slavery in Egypt. The crossing of the sea was an instance of God's miraculous intervention in their history because, without God's help, they would not have been able to rid themselves of the clutches of the Egyptians. Their escape from captivity marked a new beginning for them. In moving from slavery to freedom, they were really moving from death to new life.

The drowning of the Egyptian army after the Israelites had crossed the dry seabed became a great symbol of God's protection, just as the Israelites' successful escape symbolised God's support and faithfulness. Many centuries later, when Christianity was evolving from Judaism, the crossing of the Red Sea was recognised as prefiguring the life-giving salvation brought by Jesus Christ, which is celebrated ritually in the sacrament of baptism. For Christians, baptism is the great Easter sacrament because, in baptism, we die with Christ and are raised to the newness of his risen life. It marks a new beginning.

Water has contradictory characteristics. It gives life and it destroys life. Without water, we cannot live. Yet if there is too much water, or if it overpowers us, we may die from drowning.

Thus water can be as dangerous as it is life-giving and refreshing. These inherently contradictory characteristics are used effectively in the symbolism of baptism. The word baptism derives from a Greek verb meaning 'dipping in water'. In baptism we are washed clean of sin. We die to our former lives which have alienated us from God. Simultaneously, we are nourished and given new life by the same water. We move from death to life.

The sacrament of baptism is essentially our personal Easter event, our exodus from the oppression of sin. Living the baptised life indicates that we have been liberated and redeemed. Easter celebrates Christ's triumph over death. His resurrection from the dead is the proof that he has conquered and defeated sin.

The crossing of the Red Sea established a new beginning for the Israelites. In a sense, it facilitated their rebirth as a people. Baptism involves a spiritual rebirth for Christians. It makes us a new creation. As the Israelites crossed the Red Sea, they rejected Pharaoh and their Egyptian slave masters. They abandoned their former lives.

When we were baptised, we rejected Satan and sin. We discarded our sinful lives and we accepted the new life in Christ that God offered us. Every year, especially during the Easter Vigil, we remind ourselves of the central happenings in our salvation history and we renew our baptismal commitment. Let us pray that we will always be faithful to our baptism and rejoice that, spiritually, we have moved from death to life.

For meditation

That day, YHWH rescued Israel from the Egyptians. (Ex 14:30)

Prayer

God our Father, Creator of all,
today is the day of Easter joy.
This is the morning on which the Lord appeared to people
who had begun to lose hope
and opened their eyes to what the scriptures foretold:
that first he must die, and then he would rise
and ascend into the Father's glorious presence.
May the risen Lord
breathe on our minds and open our eyes
that we may know him in the breaking of bread,

and follow him in his risen life.
Grant this through Christ our Lord.

Second Sunday of Easter

First reading: Ac 2:42–7

Reflection
All Christians are encouraged to be clear about the church's nature. In a sense, this is an elementary matter, much as the basic arithmetical formula 2+2=4 is elementary to mathematics. But how well do all of us really know and understand the main characteristics of the church? In what way does our understanding correspond to Luke's description in the Acts of the Apostles? According to him, the essential nature of the Christian community involves remaining 'faithful to the teaching of the apostles, to the brotherhood, to the breaking of bread and to the prayers' (Ac 2:42).

Some people erroneously suggest that this vision is too idealistic. To depict a vision as idealistic implies that it is impossible to achieve because it is somehow remote from everyday reality. It is always beyond our reach. However, the Christian life is not about unachievable ideals. It is about transforming our lives and the world by being faithful to the teaching of Christ and his church. When we speak about ideals, we mean practical goals with achievable outcomes.

We need to remember that the word of God, which is inspired by God's Holy Spirit, always presents us with challenges which, although often difficult and demanding, are actually attainable with God's grace and strength. It is wrong to think otherwise. The Christian message is fundamentally practical and we cannot be half-hearted in attempting to live it.

So what relevance has Luke's account of the early Christian community for us today? Basically, it has four lessons. First, we know the church's doctrines that are communicated to us by the Magisterium (that is, teaching authority), by our Pope and bishops, who are the successors of Peter and the other apostles, and we are asked to live in conformity with them. Secondly, we are required to have a genuine concern for other people and their needs, always reaching out to them in a spirit of true charity and encouragement. Christ taught that if we give practical help to the most needy around us then we are helping him.

Thirdly and crucially, the celebration of the Eucharist must be at the heart of our lives because it nourishes us with the Body and Blood of Christ, his greatest gift to his church, while we journey towards our true home in heaven. Last, but by no means least, we are challenged to have prayerful relationships with God and with one another. This vision of the Christian community summarises the key elements of the Christian life and provides a model of the church as Christ intended it to be.

In Acts, Luke comments that the members of the Christian community were 'looked up to by everyone' and 'day by day the Lord added to their community those destined to be saved' (Ac 2:47). This was because of their humble and effective witnessing to the gospel. They were faithfully continuing Christ's mission in the world.

Unfortunately, Luke's observation about the early Christian community does not apply to much of church life today. Many of us do not live authentic Christian lives because we are not fully committed to the basic New Testament principles of living as a community of faith where the teaching of Christ is central and everyone is equally respected. It is not surprising, then, that the church is not attracting new members. Actually, it is losing many members who have become disillusioned and who no longer appreciate its relevance to their lives.

Throughout the Acts of the Apostles, the emphasis is on faithfulness to what was being handed on by the apostles. We, as members of the church, need to return to their teaching and put it into practice in our personal lives and in our faith communities. Then the church will become more credible again in its witnessing to the gospel and all people will recognise the essential characteristics of Christ's church in their midst.

For meditation
The many miracles and signs worked through the apostles made a deep impression on everyone. (Ac 2:43)

Prayer
Heavenly Father and God of mercy,
we no longer look for Jesus among the dead,
for he is alive and has become the Lord of life.
From the waters of death you raise us with him
and renew your gift of life within us.
Increase in our minds and hearts
the risen life we share with Christ
and help us to grow as your people
towards the fullness of eternal life with you.
We ask this through Christ our Lord.

Third Sunday of Easter

First reading: Ac 2:14, 22–33

Reflection
Peter and the Eleven were transformed by the resurrection of Jesus. The subsequent outpouring of the Holy Spirit changed them totally from being cowardly and despondent to being courageous and hopeful. For example, before Jesus' crucifixion and death, Peter had often been impetuous and had even denied that he knew Jesus. After the Resurrection, however, Peter and the others became confident and daring. They were not merely willing to perform, but also enthusiastic about their task of spreading the gospel throughout the world.

They were transformed into fearless and uncompromising preachers of the gospel who were certain about their task. In witnessing to the Resurrection, they challenged their listeners to open their hearts to the teaching of Jesus and to the promptings of the Holy Spirit.

What was the significance of Jesus' resurrection? It was not simply that nobody else had ever risen from the dead before. While the reality of Jesus' rising from the dead was unique and completely beyond the apostles' experiences, it became fundamentally a sign of the Father's vindication of Jesus' life and saving message. The Resurrection was (and is) living proof that bodily death is never the end, that death does not have the final victory. Jesus conquered death by giving it a new meaning. It is the gateway to eternal life.

The essential message of Peter's preaching summarised the increasingly accepted truth about Jesus. Jesus the Nazarene lived as a man who enjoyed God's blessing and support. But he was more: he was the Son of God, God's chosen Messiah. He respected the dignity of everyone and invited all people to become his disciples. He taught that the kingdom of God was nearby and urged people to change their attitudes and behaviour. He worked many miracles, including healing those who were sick and tormented. Yet he was destined to be rejected, condemned and executed. But, amazingly, by divine power he rose from the dead.

This was the mystery of Christ which, as Peter explained in his preaching, was all part of God's plan for the salvation of the world. As Peter said, it was 'by the deliberate intention and foreknowledge of God' (Ac 2:23). Peter and the Eleven spent the remainder of their lives testifying to the risen Lord Jesus and they called people to respond to God's saving love by repenting for their sins and undergoing conversion to the gospel.

The challenge to become repentant and undergo conversion is as relevant in today's world as it was during the lives of the apostles. If anything, it is more relevant. We cannot rise to the newness of Christ's risen life unless we have died to our sinful practices. This means that we cannot be credible witnesses to Jesus' resurrection from the dead unless we are also committed to his teachings and the teachings of his church.

This, of course, will make us stand out from the crowd. It may even bring us unpopularity and ridicule. We need to decide whether we wish to be like the apostles before – or after – the resurrection of Jesus from the dead. Are we cowardly instead of being committed to our faith? That is our choice as Christians in the twenty-first century.

These Easter days remind us that the risen Jesus has triumphed over suffering and death. What is the importance of the resurrection of Jesus in our lives? Like Peter and the Eleven, we are meant to be witnesses by how we live. When we are faithful to the teaching of Christ and his church, we are actively proclaiming the Resurrection and we are continuing his mission to the ends of the earth. All of us are his witnesses. Jesus has been raised from the dead. He is alive. Alleluia! Alleluia! Alleluia!

For meditation
God raised this man Jesus to life, and all of us are witnesses to that. (Ac 2:32)

Prayer
Father in heaven, author of all truth,
a people once in darkness has listened to your Word
and followed your Son as he rose from the tomb.
Hear the prayer of this newborn people
and strengthen your church to answer your call.
May we rise and come forth into the light of day
to stand in your presence until eternity dawns.
We ask this through Christ our Lord.

Fourth Sunday of Easter

First reading: Ac 2:14, 36–41

Reflection
We read in the Acts of the Apostles that when Peter and the Eleven, filled with the Holy Spirit, preached convincingly that Jesus had risen from the dead, the people were 'cut to the heart' (Ac 2:37). This means that they were deeply wounded on discovering that they had been responsible for Jesus' death. They were challenged by what they heard. So, quite understandably, they asked: 'What must we do?' (Ac 2:37)

The question 'What must we do?' was particularly significant. It acknowledged that some action was required if the listeners believed what Peter and his companions taught. It implied that serious change was necessary in their lives if they accepted the truth of the message being shared with them.

Not surprisingly, Peter replied unhesitatingly: 'You must repent' (Ac 2:38). The call to repentance had always been at the heart of Jesus' teaching, and it continued to be central to the preaching of Peter and the other apostles. The challenge to repent and undergo conversion is still fundamental to the church's mission. Action is required, sometimes radical action, because conversion is about abandoning our sinfulness and turning towards the risen Lord Jesus. Conversion to Jesus is the only way to salvation and eternal life with God in heaven.

We all need God in our lives. However, God and sin cannot coexist. Therefore, whenever we sin we are excluding – at least to some extent – God's loving presence from our lives. We are basically rejecting the teaching of Christ and his church. True repentance for our sins results in a complete change of our attitudes and behaviour so that we are faithful to the gospel message. The only appropriate Christian response to the question 'What must we do?' is 'Repent!'

There are many similarities between Peter and Pope (now Blessed) John Paul II. Both were chosen to be the chief shepherds of the church. Each of them was a fearless and uncompromising preacher of the gospel. Their words frequently caused their listeners to be 'cut to the heart', realising that, through their sins, they had contributed to the death of Jesus. Thus the question that all of us should be asking is: 'What must we do?'

People all around the world mourned the death of John Paul II. Millions were genuinely moved by his public witness to the Christian faith while he was dying and they reflected seriously on the legacy of his pontificate. Central to his own faith was the truth of the Resurrection and the daily challenge of Jesus' moral teaching. The basic lesson of his pontificate was the same as that of Peter's pontificate. Even as he was dying, if John Paul II had been asked 'What must we do?' he would have replied unambiguously 'Repent!'

There have been countless and justly deserved tributes to Pope John Paul II since his death. However, the tributes cannot be confined simply to mourning his death and admiration of him as a person. We must also learn from his teaching and example. The witness of his life and death challenges us to undergo conversion and repent for our sins. Many of us need to undergo a fundamental change of mind and heart.

For as long as there is violence, corruption and injustice in our society, and while we, as individuals, continue to sin, the world is ignoring the teaching of both Peter the Apostle and Pope John Paul II. We need instead to be 'cut to the heart' by the reality of our sins and ask 'What must we do?' We also need to listen to the answer 'Repent!'

For meditation
The whole House of Israel can be certain that God has made Jesus whom you crucified both Lord and Christ. (Ac 2:36)

Prayer
God and Father of our Lord Jesus Christ,
though your people walk in the valley of darkness,
no evil should they fear;
for they follow in faith the call of the shepherd
whom you have sent for their hope and strength.
Attune our minds to the sound of his voice,
lead our steps in the path he has shown,
that we may know the strength of his outstretched arm
and enjoy the light of your presence for ever.
We ask this in the name of Jesus the Lord.

Fifth Sunday of Easter

First reading: Ac 6:1–7

Reflection

As we read the Acts of the Apostles, we learn that, unfortunately, not everyone was treated equally in the early Christian community. Life was not always harmonious and sometimes people were marginalised for various reasons.

In one instance, the Hellenists complained that their widows were being neglected by the Hebrews. There was obvious unfairness because some members of the believing community were not cared for in the same way as others. They were actually treated like second-class citizens.

The Twelve were quite concerned when they learned about this discriminatory practice and decided that it would no longer be tolerated because it contradicted Christ's teaching. Those whose circumstances were different must not be ignored. They too were members of the Christian community and, as such, merited pastoral care. They deserved to be ministered to just as much as others, especially because ministry means service.

In appointing 'seven men of good reputation, filled with the Spirit and with wisdom' (Ac 6:3), whose specific duty was to serve the community by responding to the material needs of its members, the apostles ensured that they themselves could continue to be devoted 'to prayer and to the service of the word' (Ac 6:4). The main role of the apostles was to preach, teach and lead community worship.

However, the apostles' decision emphasised the dual roles of Christian discipleship: prayer and service. There was indeed a connection between the task of prayer and preaching and the task of distributing food and other goods to people in need. Neither role could be neglected.

There is an valuable lesson here for us. Daily prayer and regular reflection on Christian doctrines and their implications are meant to be at the centre of our everyday lives. We must understand and accept what the Christian faith is before we can practice it. We do this by praying constantly for the guidance of the Holy Spirit and by listening attentively to the church's unswerving preaching of the gospel. But we must also be willing to serve those around us who are in need. Living the gospel faithfully demands that we put other people before ourselves.

Christian discipleship challenges us to find a balance between prayer and service. Individually and collectively, we must be witnesses to the church's concern not only for the spiritual development of people but also for their material welfare, particularly if they are among the more needy members of the community. Useful service can only be sustained by genuine prayer and worship.

We need to remember that living a truly Christian lifestyle is about service born out of our love of God. It is God's love that motivates us in our service of others. Unlike non-Christians, we serve others because we see Christ in them. At baptism we are invited to become involved in the work of salvation, the vocation of building up the kingdom of God in our world. The qualities required for such apostolic work are the same as those required at the time of the Acts of the Apostles. Thus we need to ask ourselves: why might we be characterised as people of good reputations who are filled with the Holy Spirit and with wisdom? How do we understand the connection between our Christian beliefs, sustained by our prayer, and behaviour? What helps to achieve balance between prayer and service in our lives?

For meditation

They gave an account of all that God had done with them. (Ac 14:27)

Prayer

Father of our Lord Jesus Christ,
you have revealed to the nations your saving power
and filled all ages with the words of a new song.
Hear the echo of this hymn.
Give us voice to sing your praise
throughout this season of joy.
We ask this through Christ our Lord.

Sixth Sunday of Easter

First reading: Ac 8:5–8, 14–17

Reflection
We read in the Acts of the Apostles that Philip, one of the seven men chosen to assist the apostles in their ministry, went to a Samaritan town and preached the Good News about Jesus to the people there. When the apostles in Jerusalem heard that the Samaritans were 'united in welcoming the message' (Ac 8:6) Philip had preached to them and that there was 'great rejoicing in that town' (Ac 8:8) they were surprised because Jews and Samaritans had always been antagonistic towards one another. Nevertheless the Samaritans had 'accepted the word of God' (Ac 8:14).

This was so significant for the emerging church that Peter and John, two of the apostles, travelled to Samaria to complete the work begun by Philip. They prayed for the people and laid hands on them so that they would receive the Holy Spirit. Peter and John were confirming these Christian converts in their faith. The essential link between new local churches and the apostolic leadership of the church was obvious. There was remarkable unity, even though Christians were increasingly being persecuted because of their faith.

The significance of this episode in Acts was that the gospel message was spreading outside the Jewish community. It was unquestionably for all peoples. Despite rejection and persecution, the church received many new members who were united in welcoming the Good News about Jesus and salvation.

In 2005, the church and the world witnessed the election of Pope Benedict XVI, a successor of Saint Peter. Benedict and his message (which is the message of Jesus Christ) were not welcomed by those who were supposed to be united in the faith. That situation was a repetition of the one described in the Acts.

As evidenced by the worldwide televised broadcasts, millions of people welcomed Pope Benedict with great joy and enthusiasm. In contrast, most of the commentators were not fair in their reports about him. Neither were they objective in their analysis of the universal church and its message. They presented a very negative and distorted image of Benedict XVI as a church leader. Some have even suggested that the Holy Spirit made a mistake in guiding the cardinals to elect Cardinal Ratzinger as the next pope.

We need to remember that the Holy Spirit does not make mistakes. Pope Benedict's mission was the same as the mission of Peter and John in Acts. His God-given task was to preach the gospel in-season and out-of-season to a world that needed salvation. His essential role was to confirm Catholics in their faith.

More recently, we have witnessed the election of Pope Francis. At the beginning of this papacy, all Catholics are being challenged to renew their commitment to their faith and to pray for God's continued blessing on Pope Francis, who is also a successor of Peter. It is time for Catholics everywhere to be united in welcoming him and his message – which is always the message of Christ himself – and to rejoice that the Holy Spirit continues to guide the church even in the midst of rejection and, in some instances, persecution. The essential link between local churches and the apostolic leadership of the universal church needs to be restored and strengthened.

Like the first Christians, let us accept the word of God preached by the successors of Peter and let us rejoice that, through them, the Holy Spirit confirms us in our Christian faith.

For meditation
Then they laid their hands on them, and they received the Holy Spirit. (Ac 8:17)

Prayer
God our Father, maker of all,
The crown of your creation was the Son of Man,
born of a woman, but without beginning;
he suffered for us but lives for ever.
May our mortal lives be crowned with the ultimate joy
of rising with him,
who is Lord for ever and ever.

The Ascension of the Lord

First reading: Ac 1:1–11

Reflection

Occasionally, some atheists liken the Christian belief that Jesus ascended to heaven to a kind of first-century version of an outer-space mission. We are familiar with the often-used saying 'mission accomplished', which means that people, having undertaken a specific project, have achieved their goal.

This applies particularly to our thoughts about Jesus on the Feast of the Ascension, but not in the sense of a space exploration programme having been completed. Of course, atheists do not believe in the divinity of Christ, so they are unlikely to accept that he ascended to heaven at the end of his earthly life. Yet Christians affirm every time they recite the Creed that he did precisely that.

In one sense, then, the Ascension celebrates that Jesus has completed the task given to him by his Father, which, in turn, enabled him to return to the Father having done what he was sent to do: to save us from spiritual death and alienation from God because of our sins.

But in another sense, the Ascension marks the passing on of the preaching and healing ministry of Jesus to his apostles. At the beginning of his public ministry, he had preached that the kingdom of heaven was close and he had challenged people to repent and believe the Good News, which involved putting the teachings of Christ into practice in their lives. Now the responsibility for that ministry was being passed on to the apostles and disciples. They were mandated to continue his saving work, drawing all nations to the truth of the gospel.

Significantly, Jesus commissioned his disciples by saying: 'Go, therefore, make disciples of all the nations; baptise them in the name of the Father and of the Son and of the Holy Spirit, and teach them to observe all the commands I gave you. And know that I am with you always; yes, to the end of time' (Mt 28:19–20). These were his final words on earth. Anyone's final words on this earth are normally taken to be especially important. On learning of someone's death, people will often ask 'What were his/her last words?'

Jesus' ascension to the Father did not mean that the apostles and disciples would remain alone in their mission. Although he would no longer be physically present, he told them: 'You will receive power when the Holy Spirit comes on you, and then you will be my witnesses not only in Jerusalem but throughout Judaea and Samaria, and indeed to the ends of the earth' (Ac 1:8). So there was no need for them to worry or to lack confidence because he would continue to enliven and support them.

Jesus' promise to send the Holy Spirit and to remain with his church until the end of the world was an assurance that they would be guided in their various activities. In fact, we know from our experience, and the words of the risen Lord Jesus, that the church will never be alone and that it will never be abandoned by him. We celebrate that reality today as we mark the close of the post-resurrection appearances of Jesus – apart from his appearance during the conversion of Saul (see Ac 9:3–7).

The message of the Ascension is obvious. The saving work of Christ is now being handed over to the church. The task of spreading the faith to others is being passed on to us, and the responsibility for passing on the faith now rests with us. Let us carry the faith with courage and conviction and let us pass it on to those we meet.

The gift of faith, according to Jesus, has been freely given to us. Yet it comes with a price attached. Jesus' suffering and death was the price of our salvation and, consequently, when we were baptised we assumed the duty of spreading the faith. His last words on earth, immediately before his ascension to heaven, were a missionary statement instructing his followers to go into the whole world to lead people to the church. Let us pray for the grace to respond to this challenge.

For meditation

Then you will be my witnesses not only in Jerusalem but throughout Judaea and Samaria, and indeed to the ends of the earth. (Ac 1:8)

Prayer

Father in heaven,
our minds were prepared for the coming of your kingdom
when you took Christ beyond our sight

so that we might see him in his glory.
May we follow where he has led
and find our hope in his glory,
for he is Lord for ever.

Seventh Sunday of Easter

First reading: Ac 1:12–14

Reflection
We read in the Acts of the Apostles that, after Jesus had ascended to heaven, the apostles returned to the upper room and 'joined in continuous prayer' (Ac 1:14) while awaiting the outpouring of the Holy Spirit. This incident is evidence of the importance of prayer in the early Christian community and it challenges all of us in the church today to ask ourselves whether or not prayer is central in our lives and daily activities.

A relatively simple definition of prayer is that it is openness to God, openness to his life-giving and loving presence and to his providential care and will. Prayer is much more than talking to God. It is fundamentally about a personal awareness of God and behaving accordingly, glorifying God and asking him to forgive our sins and to respond to our various needs.

Notably, prayer involves listening: listening attentively to God's word and being willing to change when change is required. When we are truly open to God in prayer, our friendship with God deepens and our efforts to pray make all the difference to ourselves and the world. God, who has no needs, is not in need of our prayer. Yet he chooses to listen to us because we are in need of him.

Essentially, between Ascension and Pentecost, the apostles prepared to receive the Holy Spirit by spending significant time in prayer. During that time they undoubtedly reflected on all that Jesus had said and done, and they pondered the meaning of his message and his relevance for them. By retreating to the upper room, they were not distracted by the hustle and bustle of the crowds outside on the streets. They were able to be quiet and reflective, clarifying any confusion and doubts in their own minds and hearts. By doing so, they were better prepared to welcome the Holy Spirit.

The apostles' continuous prayer emphasises an important teaching about prayer: the need for perseverance in prayer. It is necessary that we persevere when we pray. Too often, we relate to God as if he was a magician and, consequently, we expect God to answer our prayers immediately in the way that we wish. Our focus is completely self-centred. However, sacred scripture teaches us that God does not operate according to our agenda and he does not usually work to our specific time schedules. God's ways are not our ways. Thus we need to persevere in prayer instead of impatiently abandoning it when it does not seem to be working.

Moreover, we need to persist in our prayer especially because genuine pondering and listening are necessary if we are to discover God's will and choose to be guided by the teaching of Christ and his church. We know from the gospels that Jesus, whose own prayer provides the model for all Christian prayer, persisted in his prayer, constantly discerning the Father's will for his saving mission and deepening his own relationship with the Father.

As we reflect on the Acts, among the questions we are challenged to ask ourselves are: how might we explain the importance of prayer in our lives? Why would we persist in prayer and be genuinely open to God's will? In what ways do we wholeheartedly praise God and bring our needs into his loving presence, trusting that God knows best and will always respond – even if the answer is not always the answer we expect?

For meditation

All these joined in continuous prayer, together with several women, including Mary the Mother of Jesus, and with his brothers. (Ac 1:14)

Prayer

Eternal Father,
reaching from end to end of the universe,
and ordering all things with your mighty arm:

for you, time is the unfolding of truth that already is,
the unveiling of beauty that is yet to be.
Your Son has saved us in history
by rising from the dead,
so that transcending time he might free us from death.
May his presence among us
lead to the vision of unlimited truth
and unfold the beauty of your love.
We ask this in the name of Jesus the Lord.

Pentecost Sunday

First reading (Vigil): Gn 11:1–9 or Ex 19:3–8, 16–20 or Ezk 37:1–14 or Jl 3:1–5

First reading (Mass during the Day): Ac 2:1–11

Reflection
Many people do not know that the Christian understanding of Pentecost is rooted in the Old Testament. The word Pentecost derives from the Greek word for 'fifty', referring to the fiftieth day after Jews offered the barley harvest during the feast of Passover (see Ex 34:22–3). In Old Testament times, Pentecost was also known as the Feast of Weeks because it concluded a week of weeks (forty-nine), which followed the celebration of Passover.

Later, the Acts of the Apostles records that Christ's redemptive work was completed through the coming of the Holy Spirit following his resurrection from the dead. This was the first Pentecost in the Christian sense. On that day the apostles and the other disciples were filled with the Holy Spirit and thereby transformed, becoming committed witnesses to the example of Jesus and courageous preachers of the gospel. Pentecost was the fulfilment of Jesus' promise that he would send the Holy Spirit, resulting in a powerful manifestation of the early church's faith.

The effect of the outpouring of the gifts of the Holy Spirit was miraculous. We read in Acts that, when the apostles spoke to the assembled Jews and international pilgrims, all the people heard and understood their message in their own languages. The apostles were so persuasive in their arguments that on 'that very day about three thousand were added to their number' (Ac 2:41).

It is difficult to imagine that one sermon could lead to the conversion of so many people to the gospel. Not surprisingly, this occasion emphasises the central importance of preaching the faith. Preaching is at the heart of the church's mission. The missionary activity of the church commenced on Pentecost and, beginning in Jerusalem, the gospel message was brought to Rome and gradually to the ends of the earth.

In celebrating Pentecost, we recall the descent of the Holy Spirit and the outpouring of the Spirit's gifts. The tongues of fire resting on the heads of each of them provided a visible sign of the Holy Spirit coming to assist the faith of the first Christians. This was truly a marvellous testimony to the divine assistance promised by Christ before he ascended to the Father.

We recognise that, individually and collectively, we have received various gifts of the Holy Spirit, especially in celebrating the sacrament of confirmation, when the Holy Spirit came in its fullness to transform us, as on the first Pentecost. Like the first Christian disciples, we too are helped to be faithful witnesses to the gospel and are enabled to fulfil our baptismal duty which is to proclaim and preach the Christian message to everyone we meet.

To live the Christian life, therefore, means that we live in the Holy Spirit. This involves remaining open to the Spirit's promptings. Living in the Holy Spirit demands that we abandon sin and accept completely the teaching of Christ and his church. This is fundamentally what Pentecost is about: marking the occasion when the work of salvation, through Christ's church, was – and continues to be – manifested to the world. Like the tongues of fire that descended on the heads of the first members of the church, our souls are transformed to be full of the fire of zeal to bring the truths of the faith into the lives of our families, neighbours and friends – provided that we open our souls to the Holy Spirit's guiding influence.

Pentecost reminds us once again of our need to turn away from sin and to embrace fully the teaching of Christ and his church. Let us do that with renewed enthusiasm as we pray: come, Holy Spirit, fill the hearts of your faithful and kindle in them the fire of your love. Send forth your Spirit and they shall be created. And you shall renew the face of the earth.

For meditation
We hear them preaching in our own language about the marvels of God. (Ac 2:11)

Prayer
Father of light, from whom every good gift comes,
send your Spirit into our lives
with the power of a mighty wind,
and by the flame of your wisdom
open the horizons of our minds.
Loosen our tongues to sing your praise
in words beyond the power of speech,
for without your Spirit
human beings could never raise their voices in words of peace
or announce the truth that Jesus is Lord,
who lives and reigns with you and the Holy Spirit,
one God, for ever and ever.

Selected Feasts of the Lord in Ordinary Time

The Most Holy Trinity

First reading: Ex 34:4–6, 8–9

Reflection

We do not often think explicitly about the Mystery of the Trinity. In that respect, we are really not so different from most preceding generations of Christians who, while usually not focusing particular attention on the Trinity, were nevertheless steeped in its mystery in many aspects of daily Christian living.

For example, Catholics routinely make the sign of the cross whenever they begin to pray, by saying, 'In the name of the Father, and of the Son, and of the Holy Spirit.' In this they are articulating the most fundamental Christian belief – that there are three distinct Persons (Father and Son and Holy Spirit) in one God. The Father is not the Son, the Son is not the Holy Spirit, and the Holy Spirit is not the Father or the Son. Each Person is distinct from the other two.

In making the sign of the cross and in saying the accompanying words, Catholics – and other Christians – are not only affirming their belief in God who is Father and Son and Holy Spirit, they are also linking the significance of the death of Jesus Christ on the cross with the Triune God. Thus we profess our belief that Jesus was truly God and truly human.

Similarly, the opening prayer of the Mass and the concluding prayer of the church's Morning and Evening Prayer typically conclude with the phrase: 'Through our Lord Jesus Christ, your Son, who lives and reigns with you [Father] in the unity of the Holy Spirit, one God, for ever and ever.' Those present answer 'Amen', meaning that they agree with what the presiding bishop, priest or deacon has just prayed in their name and on their behalf. Thus they freely and deliberately acknowledge the Trinitarian nature of God.

Although it requires a combination of Scripture (both the Old and New Testaments) and Tradition (that is, the lived faith experience), to formulate the doctrine of the Trinity, there are hints about the nature of God in the Old Testament. For example, in the Book of Exodus we read that Moses addressed God as follows: 'YHWH, YHWH, a God of tenderness and compassion, slow to anger, rich in kindness and faithfulness' (Ex 34:6). Moses went even further when he continued: 'If I have indeed won your favour, Lord, let my Lord come with us, I beg. True, they are a headstrong people, but forgive us our faults and our sins, and adopt us as your heritage' (Ex 34:8–9). Again, this offers a hint about the nature of God.

The ability and willingness of Moses to talk to God with such conversational familiarity is evidence that, for all of God's transcendence, he is a personal God who is available to his people and willing to listen to their intercessions. Furthermore, the fact that Moses was able to describe God as being tender and compassionate, slow to anger and rich in kindness, demonstrates that God is amenable to the plight of his people and actively involved in caring for them. All of this, when added to similar evidence gathered from other parts of the Bible, provides a starting point for formulating the doctrine of the Trinity: God is Three and God is One.

This belief is incomprehensible for human beings. It simply does not make sense. How can one be three and three be one? As we argue in basic mathematics, 'Three into one does not go!' Yet God's revelation (that is, self-communication) to us is precisely that. It is a mystery – the greatest of all mysteries – that, like all other mysteries, invites us to ponder it, thereby participating in it and appreciating it without necessarily understanding it fully.

But this does not mean that there is no answer to the mystery of God. There is at least a partial answer. We are dealing with supernatural reality. Hence we cannot comprehend the ways and things of God fully in this world. However, we do not have to understand fully in order to believe. We know that God's revelation must be true because God cannot lie. The revelation of the scriptures is unmistakable and the tradition of the Christian faith is unambiguous.

As we celebrate the Feast of the Most Holy Trinity, let us make our own the words of the opening prayer of the Mass: God our Father, who by sending into the world the Word of truth and the Spirit of sanctification made known to the human race your wondrous mystery, grant us, we pray, that in professing the true faith, we may acknowledge the Trinity of eternal glory and adore your Unity, powerful in majesty. Through our Lord Jesus Christ, your Son, who lives and reigns with you in the unity of the Holy Spirit, one God, for ever and ever.

For meditation
YHWH, YHWH, a God of tenderness and compassion, slow to anger, rich in kindness and faithfulness. (Ex 34:6)

Prayer
God, we praise you:
Father all-powerful, Christ Lord and Saviour, Spirit of love.
You reveal yourself in the depths of our being,
drawing us to share in your life and your love.
One God, three Persons,
be near to the people formed in your image,
close to the world your love brings to life.
We ask you this, Father and Son and Holy Spirit,
one God, true and living, for ever and ever.

The Body and Blood of Christ

First reading: Dt 8:2–3, 14–16

Reflection
In celebrating the Feast of Corpus Christi (that is, the Body and Blood of Christ) the church presents us with a timely opportunity to reflect on the meaning and significance of the Eucharist in our lives. The Mass is at the centre of our Catholic faith because, according to the teaching of the Church Fathers, the Eucharist makes the church. Thus the Eucharist and the church are inextricably linked. We cannot have the church without the Eucharist. Neither can we have the Eucharist without the church.

Catholics believe that, during the celebration of Mass, the bread and wine are transformed into the Body and Blood, Soul and Divinity of Christ. Therefore, in Holy Communion we receive Christ, whole and entire, under the appearance of bread and wine – because he is really and truly present under the appearance of bread and wine that have become his Body and Blood. During the Eucharistic Prayer, before the priest says the words of institution he invokes the Holy Spirit to change the bread and wine into the Body and Blood of Christ.

Then, after the words of institution, the priest invokes the Holy Spirit a second time. This time the invocation is to change all those who are present at Mass into the Body of Christ. Sometimes, however, we are oblivious to this powerful request because we have become so used to hearing the words of the Eucharistic Prayer that we daydream and take them for granted.

Yet the phrases in the Eucharistic Prayers are so meaningful: 'so that all of us, who through this participation at the altar receive the most holy Body and Blood of your Son, may be filled with every grace and heavenly blessing' (Eucharistic Prayer 1); 'humbly we pray that, partaking of the Body and Blood of Christ, we may be gathered into one by the Holy Spirit' (Eucharistic Prayer 2); 'grant that we, who are nourished by the Body and Blood of your Son and filled with his Holy Spirit, may become one body, one spirit in Christ' (Eucharistic Prayer 3); 'and grant in your loving kindness to all who partake of this one Bread and one Chalice that, gathered into one body by the Holy Spirit, they may truly become a living sacrifice in Christ to the praise of your glory' (Eucharistic Prayer 4).

These phrases are evocative of the Book of Deuteronomy where Moses reminded the people that God had fed and nourished them for forty years while they wandered through the wilderness: 'He [God] fed you with manna which neither you nor your fathers had known, to make you understand that man does not live on bread alone but that man lives on everything that comes from the mouth of YHWH' (Dt 8:3). Christians have long understood these words as prefiguring the bread from heaven that Christ would give us in the Eucharist. The manna in the wilderness satisfied the physical hunger of the Israelites. However, their spiritual hunger could only be satisfied by the word of God.

Our duty, as members of the church – the Body of Christ – is to nourish our souls by our interior participation at Mass and by receiving Holy Communion – our spiritual manna and food from heaven – regularly so that we are strengthened, spiritually, in order to live our Catholic lives fully with our families and in our workplaces and schools. On the Feast of Corpus Christi, then, let us pray that we will always respond wholeheartedly to the abiding presence of Christ in the Eucharist. Let us also pray that we will be continually transformed into the Mystical Body of Christ.

For meditation

He fed you with manna which neither you nor your fathers had known, to make you understand that man does not live on bread alone but that man lives on everything that comes from the mouth of YHWH. (Dt 8:3)

Prayer

Lord Jesus Christ,
we worship you living among us
in the sacrament of your body and blood.
May we offer to our Father in heaven
a solemn pledge of undivided love.
May we offer to our brothers and sisters
a life poured out in loving service of that kingdom
where you live with the Father and the Holy Spirit,
one God, for ever and ever.

Sundays in Ordinary Time

Second Sunday in Ordinary Time

First reading: Is 49:3, 5–6

Reflection
In the prophecy of the Book of Isaiah, God indicated that the servant who would come into the world would be the light of the nations. God said: 'It is not enough for you to be my servant, to restore the tribes of Jacob and bring back the survivors of Israel; I will make you the light of the nations so that my salvation may reach to the ends of the earth' (Is 49:6).

It is obvious from this prophecy that the servant to whom God referred was different from other servants. He was chosen by God, even before his birth, for the unique task of bringing God's salvation to all peoples. Although the people of Israel were God's Chosen People, God did not wish to confine salvation to them alone. He wanted everyone to be saved because all people from every time and nationality, being created in God's image and likeness, reflect aspects of God's truth and awesomeness.

Eventually, the prophecy about the servant was fulfilled in Jesus, the Word made flesh. At Christmas we celebrated his entry into human history as the Messiah – the Saviour sent by God because of God's infinite love for the world. Jesus was the light of the nations, bringing God's love and mercy to the pagans and gentiles as well as to the Jews. He proved by his words and behaviour that redemption is not only for the Jewish people. He actively invited people to become his disciples. He taught them to be the salt of the earth and the light of the world.

Jesus' task was indeed missionary. He was sent by the Father with a definite purpose, which was to restore God's creation to its original perfection. He did this by enabling people to experience the nearness of God's kingdom through his teaching and miracles and by challenging them to repent of their sins and undergo conversion to his way of living. He made the ultimate sacrifice when he died on the cross to save all people from the consequences of sin. Thus Jesus was truly the Suffering Servant who was the light of the nations.

The risen, glorified Jesus scattered the darkness of sin and death. He was truly the light of the nations. His essential message was one of universal salvation and he commissioned his apostles and disciples to continue preaching and teaching that message until his return at the end of time.

The church, which consists of all those who are baptised, exists so that God's salvation in Jesus Christ may be brought to the ends of the earth. It is often described as 'the new Israel' because it is the means of salvation for all nationalities. It is the sign on earth of God's salvation. That is why we believe that the church is necessary for salvation. Just as Christ is necessary for salvation so also is the church, which is the Body of Christ, even for those who do not belong.

Each of us, as members of the church, is called to become the light of the nations. This means that we must be serious about our faith and practise it as best we can in our daily lives, especially when we have to make decisions that do not conform to the prevailing culture in society that so often contravenes God's commandments. In this way we imitate the Suffering Servant, we engage in the church's mission and, with Christ as our head, we collectively become the light of the nations.

For meditation
I will make you the light of the nations so that my salvation may reach to the ends of the earth. (Is 49:6)

Prayer
Almighty and ever-present Father,
your watchful care reaches from end to end
and orders all things in such power
that even the tensions and the tragedies of sin
cannot frustrate your loving plans.
Help us to embrace your will,
give us the strength to follow your call,
so that your truth may live in our hearts
and reflect peace to those who believe in you.
We ask this in the name of Jesus the Lord.

Third Sunday in Ordinary Time

First reading: Is 8:23 – 9:3

Reflection

Most of us are quite familiar with these famous words from the Book of Isaiah: 'The people that walked in darkness has seen a great light; on those who live in a land of deep shadow a light has shone' (Is 9:1). What beautiful and encouraging words!

We listen to them being proclaimed, as part of a wonderful prophecy, every Christmas during the celebration of Midnight Mass. Many of us can probably recite them from memory because they are among the most compassionate and inspiring words in the Bible.

The prophet who spoke these words was reminding his audience that they could always have hope, knowing that God was with them through all their afflictions and especially while they were in exile. However, the future would be glorious because they would be freed from exile and would experience no more hardship.

A brilliant light would shine on them and liberate them from the surrounding darkness. Their lives would never be the same again. Actually, the prophet's words were so enthusiastic that it was as if this change had already occurred. It was as though the future had arrived. Such was the prophet's hope.

The prophet foretold the future coming of God's Messiah who would be a descendant of King David. That prophecy was fulfilled at the birth of Jesus, the Word made flesh. Jesus established a kingdom of justice, peace and love. He was the living proof of God's unconditional love. His life, death and resurrection brought salvation from sin, and hope for eternity.

Unfortunately, many people in today's world are living in various kinds of psychological, emotional and spiritual darkness. It may be the darkness of despair and loneliness, confusion and depression. Or it may be the darkness of violence and injustice, suffering and tragedy. The worst kind of darkness, however, is sin because it destroys the light and life of Christ in our lives. This is particularly true of people whose consciences are dead because they never engage with the teaching of Christ and his church. Thus Isaiah's message about God's salvation is arguably needed more now than at any time in the past.

All of us need to turn towards Christ and the church, especially if we are unrepentant sinners. Sin invariably brings spiritual darkness, but we do not always recognise its harmful effects in our friendships with God. Many people are so enslaved to sin that they cannot experience lasting happiness – although they may experience some transient pleasure and satisfaction. Sincerely and humbly celebrating the sacrament of reconciliation would offer them God's grace that is necessary for conversion and true peace.

The gospel challenges us to abandon sin and to teach others to do the same. There is only one way to scatter darkness and that is to allow the light to shine brightly. Christ is our light, the Lamb of God who takes away the sins of the world.

Realising that God loves us, we should be shaken out of our complacency. Can we easily say that we are hopeful people in all circumstances? How do we share a message of hope with those around us who are hopeless? In what ways do we help those who walk in darkness to see the light of Christ?

Our faith challenges us to be like the prophet Isaiah, speaking and living with the conviction that we receive from our relationship with God – a relationship that is free from unrepentant sin and completely open to doing God's will so that we can truly rejoice in God's presence.

For meditation

The people that walked in darkness has seen a great light; on those who live in a land of deep shadow a light has shone. (Is 9:1)

Prayer

The love you offer
always exceeds the furthest expression of our human longing,
for you are greater than the human heart.
Direct each thought, each effort of our life,
so that the limits of our faults and weaknesses
may not obscure the vision of your glory
or keep us from the peace you have promised.
We ask this through Christ our Lord.

Fourth Sunday in Ordinary Time

First reading: Zp 2:3; 3:12–13

Reflection
What is authentic poverty, at least according to the biblical understanding? Contrary to what many people think, it is not limited to (although it often includes) the absence of money and material possessions. Instead, it is fundamentally an attitude of detachment from people and possessions, but even more an attitude of humility before God, whereby we decide not to make ourselves the sole focus in any relationship or situation and not to be disrespectful towards other people even when we have different beliefs.

The opposite of such an attitude is arrogance. Arrogance makes us self-righteous and gives us a false sense of self-importance. When we are arrogant, everyone diminishes in importance. We assume that we are superior to them and that they are only a means to our end rather than ends in themselves. We use them to our own selfish advantage without any genuine concern for their interests and well-being. For example, we tell them lies and we manipulate them so that we win the argument. Understandably, these people avoid us because experience has taught them that we exploit them.

Similarly, in our relationships with God, arrogance leads us to think that we can exist without him and that his commandments are irrelevant. For example, we do not bother to pray to God and develop a loving relationship with him. It is not surprising, then, that pride is frequently described as the most basic sin. Arrogance corrupts us and prevents us from appreciating the need for repentance and, consequently, alienates us from God and from other people.

We need to remember that true happiness cannot be found in worldly possessions or in personal fame. Real poverty of spirit and sincere humility are found only in those who know their absolute dependence on God. The problem is that arrogance stops us from recognising this. Thus there is the need for a regular self-examination of conscience and the frequent celebration of the sacrament of penance.

Significantly, the prophet Zephaniah offered hope to his contemporaries who were exploited by proud and self-centred people. He encouraged them to be humble in the biblical sense. In other words, they were lowly and poor in spirit as well as materially.

According to Zephaniah, the poor are those who seek the Lord, humbly obeying his commandments while doing no wrong and telling no lies. They are people who believe in God's offer of salvation and live in the hope of achieving that salvation. Therefore, their focus is on finding God in this life as a preparation for finding him in the next life.

Poverty is essentially an attitude of detachment from people and the things of this world, not because they are bad in themselves but because, if not valued and used properly, they may hinder us in our search for the real wealth that only God can give. It is about abandoning ourselves completely to God's will, accepting that our riches will come from him rather than acquiring them for ourselves.

Ironically, it is possible for people who are materially poor to be arrogant and self-righteous, which contradicts the biblical understanding of poverty. The questions being asked of us by the word of God today include: how are we poor in the biblical sense? Why would we acknowledge our total dependence on God? In what ways do we keep his commandments? Is it helpful for us to be repentant for the times we have been self-righteous and proud? How do we demonstrate our respect for other people?

All of us need to grow in our reliance on God and in our desire to do God's will. Then, and only then, will we discover the true meaning of poverty and humility.

For meditation

In your midst I will leave a humble and lowly people. (Zp 3:12)

Prayer

Father in heaven,
from the days of Abraham and Moses
until this gathering of your church in prayer,
you have formed a people in the image of your Son.
Bless this people with the gift of your kingdom.

May we serve you with our every desire
and show love for one another
even as you have loved us.
Grant this through Christ our Lord.

Fifth Sunday in Ordinary Time

First reading: Is 58:7–10

Reflection
We all like to be treated well and we are usually disappointed if other people ignore us when we need their help and encouragement. Thus the Golden Rule for everyday living is: treat others as you would like them to treat you. Furthermore, one of the basic principles of Christian living is: the first will be last and the last will be first.

The prophet Isaiah preached with this conviction. God spoke through him and said to the people: 'Share your bread with the hungry, and shelter the homeless poor, clothe the man you see to be naked and turn not away from your own kin' (Is 58:7). Do these words not remind us of some of Jesus' words in the Sermon on the Mount (see Mt 5–7)?

The message is obvious. We cannot separate religious beliefs and devotional practices from our responsibility to be genuinely concerned for others. As Christians, we must care primarily for their spiritual needs but also, of course, their material well-being. If our profession of faith does not influence our behaviour, we are hypocrites and hypocrisy is a sin. History is often repeated, because this message needs to be learned just as much today as at any time in the past.

Our behaviour must be inspired by correctly formed attitudes and dispositions. This means that there has to be consistency between what we say and what we do. We cannot seriously claim to have a loving relationship with God unless we try to see Christ in those around us. This is particularly true in our society which has become so prosperous and materialistic. We should remember that, in feeding the hungry, we are caring for Christ himself.

The word of God challenges us to be kind and generous to those who are less privileged than ourselves. On the world stage, there is always great evidence of compassion and self-giving in terms of material giving in the aftermath of appalling natural disasters. People on every continent donate huge amounts of money to charity and aid agencies so that the suffering of countless victims can be alleviated. Even more importantly, there is a tremendous outpouring of prayer, asking God to be merciful to those who had died and to comfort and console those who survived.

Then, on a less dramatic level locally, there is, for example, the untiring ministry of the members of the Society of Saint Vincent de Paul. These men and women are volunteers who help people in need and make a real difference in their lives. Unfortunately, however, many of us rarely inconvenience ourselves for the benefit and welfare of needy people.

At the heart of the gospel is the invitation – and indeed the challenge – to do the 'corporal works of mercy'. That is also what Isaiah exhorted his people to do. We can do these works without necessarily joining a charitable organisation or an overseas aid agency. We need only observe those around us and respond with a generous heart to their difficulties and needs. We need to learn again to see Christ in them.

God tells us, speaking through Isaiah: 'If you do away with the yoke, the clenched fist, the wicked word, if you give your bread to the hungry, and relief to the oppressed, your light will rise in the darkness and your shadows become like noon' (Is 58:9–10). Salvation depends on how we live in the here and now. Surely there is nothing further to be said!

For meditation
Then will your light shine like the dawn. (Is 58:8)

Prayer
In faith and love we ask you, Father,
to watch over your family gathered here.
In your mercy and loving kindness

no thought of ours is left unguarded,
no tear unheeded, no joy unnoticed.
Through the prayer of Jesus
may the blessings promised to the poor in spirit
lead us to the treasures of your heavenly kingdom.
We ask this in the name of Jesus the Lord.

Sixth Sunday in Ordinary Time

First reading: Si 15:15–20

Reflection
We need to be cautious when interpreting the underlying message contained in any given extract from the Bible, in the sense that we need to read and understand it in its proper context. Otherwise, our interpretation could easily be inaccurate and misleading. In practice, this means that it is inadvisable to take a particular verse in isolation; rather it must be considered in the context of the Bible in its entirety.

A good example of a biblical phrase that, on its own, could be misunderstood, is found in the Book of Sirach (also known as Ecclesiasticus): 'If you wish, you can keep the commandments, to behave faithfully is within your power' (Si 15:15). An initial approach to interpreting this phrase might suggest that we are autonomous beings who can achieve all our desires – including saving ourselves – without any reliance on God.

Such an understanding would be wrong because it denies our dependence on God. If we read the preceding part of chapter 15 of Sirach, we quickly familiarise ourselves with the context and realise that we depend totally on God for life and salvation from the consequences of our sins. Nevertheless, God has given us the gift of free will, which enables us to choose to live according to his commandments or to disregard them.

So, at least to that extent, we are in control of our ultimate destiny. This means that we are in charge of our lives, but only because God has given us the freedom to make choices and decisions that will determine our final destiny. God never compels us to act in accordance with his commandments – although he constantly makes it clear that his will is for us to allow them to enable us to live as he intended. Instead, God offers us various alternatives because he fundamentally respects the freedom he has given us. Another phrase from Sirach exemplifies this: 'Man has life and death before him; whichever a man likes better will be given him' (Si 15:17). In other words, the moral choices we make in this life will determine our eternal fate.

As strange as it may seem, God's commandments are given to enable us to enjoy and celebrate life to the fullest, to be at our happiest and most fulfilled. When we think about them objectively, we recognise the wisdom that lies at the heart of each commandment. The only logical conclusion is that there is no happiness, as distinct from short-lived pleasure, without obedience to God's commandments. Obedience, in the biblical sense, is nothing more or less than listening to the voice of God, which is also present in many forms in addition to the commandments. Obedience is not to be understood in the military sense of carrying out orders. The commandments are not just guides to a good life. They are instructions on how to live a healthy life, both physically and spiritually.

If we could only learn this essential truth early in life, we would avoid many of the hardships that inevitably cross our path. But that is a consequence of how we use the freedom that God has given us. Many people forget that freedom brings great responsibility. Once again, the words of Sirach are appropriate: '[God] never commanded anyone to be godless, he has given no one permission to sin' (Si 15:20).

The fundamental lesson here is that God has given us free will so that we may choose him and his law. We are physically, but not morally, free to choose sin. But if we choose sin, we cannot justify it by claiming that we are exercising our free will. God gave us free will so that we may freely choose good over evil.

Therefore, let us pray that we will appreciate the gift of free will. And let us pray that we will begin to appreciate the grace and strength God gives us to be faithful to his commandments. Only when we humbly and graciously accept God's grace will we be able to exercise our free will in ways that acknowledge our complete dependence on God for all that we have. God never asks us to do anything that is impossible.

For meditation
He never commanded anyone to be godless, he has given no one permission to sin. (Si 15:20)

Prayer
Father in heaven,
the loving plan of your wisdom took flesh in Jesus Christ,
and changed humankind's history
by his command of perfect love.
May our fulfilment of his command reflect your wisdom
and bring salvation to the ends of the earth.
We ask this through Chris our Lord.

Seventh Sunday in Ordinary Time

First reading: Lv 19:1–2, 17–18

Reflection
The Catholic Church has always taught that its members are called to holiness. One important instance is found in a document from the Second Vatican Council that presents the church's self-understanding. That document, usually known as *Lumen Gentium* (meaning 'light of the nations') has a chapter entitled 'The universal call to holiness'. Thus we can confidently presume that holiness is at the heart of the church's life and a major characteristic of the Christian way of life.

Interestingly, in the Old Testament, there are several instances of a clear mandate from God to be holy. For example, in the Book of Leviticus God instructed Moses to tell the people: 'Be holy, for I, YHWH your God, am holy' (Lv 19:2). We already know from God's self-disclosure, as recorded in various places in the Bible, that God is all-loving, eternal, omnipotent (that is, all-powerful) and omniscient (that is, all-knowing). Now, in addition to these attributes, we know that God is also holy. And, significantly, we are called to be holy because God is holy.

So what, then, does holiness really mean? Perhaps the best definition of it, as God's own words suggest, is that it is the imitation of God (in Latin, *imitatio Dei*). This understanding of holiness is further elaborated by Jesus himself when he exhorts his disciples to 'be perfect just as your heavenly Father is perfect' (Mt 5:48). Of course, it is important to understand that such striving for perfection is not intended to lead to neuroticism.

In Leviticus, God implies that there is a connection between being holy and being faithful to his commandments. He challenges us to 'love' our neighbour and not to 'bear hatred', 'exact vengeance' or 'bear a grudge' (Lv 19:17–18). If being holy is imitating God and involves these challenges, this means that a true image of God is one in which God is understood and experienced as loving and not hateful, vengeful or grudging. This, then, is the image of God that we are called to reflect in our lives. The imitation of God necessarily involves the avoidance of sin because imitating God and committing sin are incompatible.

Achieving holiness is a lifelong task. It does not happen overnight, but requires much work and effort. It involves continuously trying to act as God acts. God's holiness is based on love, as is the moral life. Therefore, if we are to become holy as God is holy, we need to become people who love God and our neighbour as ourselves.

Saint Francis de Sales (1567–1622) once said: 'All of us can attain to Christian virtue and holiness, no matter in what condition of life we live and no matter what our life-work may be.' The implication is that holiness is not restricted, for example, to those called to priesthood and religious life. Neither is it restricted to those who are wealthy or poor, nor to those who have status in society. The fact is that God calls everyone to holiness, and that is why the Catholic Church includes the notion of the universal call to holiness in its major teaching document on its self-understanding.

For meditation

You must love your neighbour as yourself. (Lv 19:18)

Prayer
Almighty God,
Father of our Lord Jesus Christ,
faith in your word is the way to wisdom,
and to ponder your divine plan is to grow in the truth.
Open our eyes to your deeds,
our ears to the sound of your call,
so that our every act may increase our sharing
in the life you have offered us.
Grant this through Christ our Lord.

Eighth Sunday in Ordinary Time

First reading: Is 49:14–15

Reflection
The comparison of God's love for each one of us to that of a mother's love for her 'baby at the breast' (Is 49:15) is indeed a beautiful and tender image.

We instinctively know that it is against a mother's nature for her to abandon and forget her baby. It is a biological fact that the bond between a mother and her infant is one of the strongest of all bonds, because her baby has already lived in her womb before birth. Just as a mother's womb provides a safe place for her baby to grow and develop, so the mother continues to provide warmth, shelter, nourishment and protection after her baby's birth. The infant is helpless and completely dependent on the mother for life and sustenance. Thus it is no wonder that such a strong attachment develops between mother and child.

A mother is willing to sacrifice her own desires and comforts to ensure that her child is happy and safe. Even after the death of an adult child, it is quite normal for that child's mother (if she is still alive) to be broken-hearted and grief-stricken, because part of her own life – that she nurtured so lovingly – has been taken away from her. That is why it is only in the rarest and most unusual circumstances that a mother would freely abandon, mistreat or forget her child. Regrettably, however, this happens occasionally.

In contrast, the reality is that God never abandons us and never forgets us. As improbable as it sounds that a mother would forget her child, it is impossible that God would do so – such is his perfect and unconditional love. God always shares his life with us by drawing us into his own life. Paradoxically, although God loves each one of us equally, he also loves each one of us uniquely. But that is not surprising because, as we often read in the Bible, nothing is impossible to God.

God gives us life and sustains us. He protects us from harm and evil, and he guides and directs us as we journey towards our true home in heaven. He has established a covenant with us because we are his Chosen People. He is always faithful to that covenant and never abandons us. Although we often desert God by our sinful behaviour, he is like a mother who cannot ignore the plight of her child and who waits patiently for her child to return. Like a mother, too, God continually reaches out to us offering us another chance.

We are familiar with the idea of God's fatherly love since that is how God's love is predominantly portrayed through the pages of the Bible. However, we are less used to the idea of God's motherly love. Yet the tender bond that characterises the motherly aspect of God's love is as real, meaningful and relevant as any of the fatherly aspects of God's love. In presenting such images of God's love, the prophet Isaiah makes a clear statement about the enduring love that God has for all his people. God never leaves us; he is always at our side.

The words of 'You'll Never Walk Alone', from the 1945 Rodgers and Hammerstein musical *Carousel*, summarise Isaiah's message about God:

> When you walk through a storm
> hold your head up high,
> and don't be afraid of the dark.
>
> At the end of the storm
> there's a golden sky,
> and the sweet silver song of the lark.

Walk on through the wind,
walk on through the rain,
though your dreams be tossed and blown.
Walk on, walk on, with hope in your heart,
for you'll never walk alone.
You'll never walk alone.

When God is with us, we never walk alone!

For meditation
I will never forget you. (Is 49:15)

Prayer
Father in heaven,
form in us the likeness of your Son
and deepen his life within us.
Send us as witnesses of gospel joy
into a world of fragile peace and broken promises.
Touch the hearts of all people with your love
that they in turn may love one another.
We ask this through Christ our Lord.

Ninth Sunday in Ordinary Time

First reading: Dt 11:18, 26–8, 32

Reflection
The commandments of God are at the heart of both the Jewish and Christian faiths because they exemplify the terms of the covenant relationship established between God and the Israelites and also because of Christ's words: 'If you love me you will keep my commandments' (Jn 14:15). The commandments specify the basic moral behaviours and ritual practices that God requires. Fundamentally, they form the charter of what it means to live as God's Chosen People.

Jesus' moral teaching is best summarised in the Sermon on the Mount (see Mt 5–7), also referred to as the Sermon on the Plain (see Lk 6). Yet he insisted that he had not come to abolish the Law and the Prophets. Instead, he came to fulfil them. He developed them further. Therefore, the various commandments in the Old Testament and the moral principles they espouse are relevant for Christians in today's world.

God's commandments provide us with definite instructions for everyday living. They emphasise the need for correct and respectful relationships with God and with one another. They teach us that we cannot separate our relationship with God from our various relationships with other people. This means that we cannot have a straightforward 'vertical' relationship with God without also having a 'horizontal' relationship with God through our relationships with the people we meet in everyday life.

The fundamental message of God's commandments is that we must love God and our neighbour. Christians cannot love one without the other. We cannot legitimately compartmentalise God and people such that they remain unconnected. Thus our dealings with others have implications for our friendship with God.

Nowadays, many people dismiss God's commandments as being irrelevant to modern life. They are often viewed negatively because they seem to be imposing limitations on our freedom. However, we need to remember the context in which the Israelites received them from God. They received the commandments having escaped from slavery in Egypt and having begun to live freely in the presence of God who cared for them. Contrary to popular opinion, the purpose of the commandments was to enable them to appreciate the freedom of living according to God's will. It was undoubtedly not to make their lives miserable.

Similarly, God's commandments demand obedience as we respond faithfully to God's will in our lives. They summarise what is required in order to live a wholesome life that reflects God's truth and beauty. Their purpose is to rid our lives of selfishness and self-centredness so that we can learn to put God and other people first and ourselves last. When our consciences are informed by the commandments, as the church teaches, we know the difference between right and wrong. Living according to God's commandments ensures true happiness which is much deeper than the many fleeting pleasures of our time.

The Book of Deuteronomy teaches us about the commandments in the context of blessings and curses. It makes clear that, if we keep the commandments and live according to them, we will be blessed. But if we disobey them and refuse to live by them, we will be cursed.

God's commandments provide us with an appropriate examination of conscience so that we can recognise the areas in our lives that need conversion. Let us, therefore, appreciate them as gifts from God which, when we live in obedience to them, lead us to a truly liberating way of life that guarantees genuine happiness in this life and eternal happiness in heaven.

For meditation
See, I set before you today a blessing and a curse. (Dt 11:26)

Prayer
God our Father,
teach us to cherish the gifts that surround us.
Increase our faith in you
and bring our trust to its promised fulfilment
in the joy of your kingdom.
Grant this through Christ our Lord.

Tenth Sunday in Ordinary Time

First reading: Ho 6:3–6

Reflection
How well to we know God? More fundamentally, what does it mean to claim that we know God? There are different types of knowledge, and understanding the differences between them has implications for how we use our knowledge in everyday life.

There is an important difference between knowing about a person and knowing that person personally. We often know many facts and anecdotes about a particular person (for example, Pope Francis, Queen Elizabeth II, President Barack Obama) without ever having met that person or without having ever experienced living and working alongside him / her.

However, such information without a real relationship is always deficient. In the absence of meaningful friendship, our knowledge is usually quite superficial because a mere intellectual acquaintance is always less complete than being united through a trusting and respectful intimacy.

During the eighth century before the coming of Christ, the prophet Hosea said to the Israelites: 'Let us set ourselves to know YHWH' (Ho 6:3). Hosea was not suggesting that the people learn more about God. Rather, he was recommending that they begin to know God personally. Knowing God personally would make all the difference.

It would involve listening to God's voice, especially when God was speaking to them through the prophets. It would demand that they make a commitment which had obligations and responsibilities. It would require that they change their lifestyles to mirror, instead, the perfect love that can be found only in God.

Hosea supported his recommendation by reminding the Israelites about God's commitment to them. He said 'that he will come is as certain as the dawn, his judgement will rise like the light, he will come to us as showers come' (Ho 6:3). Hosea, speaking for God, added, 'what I want is love, not sacrifice; knowledge of God, not holocausts' (Ho 6:6). In other words, God desired genuine love and commitment instead of empty ritual and hypocrisy. Of course, this does not mean that God did not want sacrifices. We need to remember that love, properly understood, essentially embraces sacrifice.

According to Hosea – and, indeed, all the biblical prophets – true knowledge of God could only be claimed if people were living in a faithful relationship with God. This involves fidelity to the commandments. Obedience is the only way to establish a genuine friendship with God.

Long after Hosea, God proved that he loved the world and all its peoples so much that he sent his only Son into the world to save us from the consequences of our sins. Jesus founded the church to continue his saving mission after he returned to the Father. Today the church continues in the tradition of Hosea and the other great prophets, continually calling people to repentance and conversion.

The church is the vehicle through which we know Jesus personally. We meet him uniquely and intimately especially when we celebrate the sacraments and when we pray to him. Through our personal relationships with Jesus we develop a friendship and intimacy with God our heavenly Father, remembering the words of Jesus: 'To have seen me is to have seen the Father' (Jn 14:9).

When we know Jesus personally, we begin to know the Father personally, rather than merely acquiring information about him. To know God truly is the goal of our lives on this earth.

For meditation
What I want is love, not sacrifice. (Ho 6:6)

Prayer
Father in heaven,
words cannot measure the boundaries of love
for those born to new life in Christ Jesus.
Raise us beyond the limits this world imposes,
so that we may be free to love as Christ teaches
and find our joy in your glory.
We ask this through Christ our Lord.

Eleventh Sunday in Ordinary Time

First reading: Ex 19:2–6

Reflection
People sometimes have strange and false images of God. Some people feel that God is to be feared, that God and his church deliberately make life difficult and unnecessarily demanding. Consequently, they live in fear of God, they are often scrupulous and are unable to enjoy life. Other people are inclined not to be

serious about God at all. They believe that it does not really matter how we live; God loves us anyway and does not make any demands. For many people, too, God seems to be remote and unapproachable. They perceive God as being indifferent. They are convinced that they do not matter to God.

Yet the truth is in stark contrast to such false images of God and is unmistakable: we are most assuredly God's people and it is because God loves us and wants what is best for us that he is often demanding and challenging. We belong to God.

In the Book of Exodus, God reminded the Israelites – his Chosen People – that they were very precious. In fact, he loved them so much that he had liberated them from slavery and exile in Egypt. He had saved them from the cruelties and humiliations being inflicted by the Egyptians. God had chosen the Israelites (those whom others would have least expected) to be his own people.

As God communicated with them through their leader, Moses, they had the opportunity to recognise God's compassion. God had shown great care. It emerged that there was no reason to fear God because God was always on their side – if only they could accept it and believe. However, God expected his people to be faithful and loyal to him. Their relationship was a two-way relationship. There were implications for God's people in this relationship. These were that they obey God's voice and hold fast to his covenant. Such were the demands God made as he established a alliance with the Israelites as his people.

We need to remember that, as members of God's people in Christ's church, we are the descendants of the Israelites who escaped from Egypt. Although we live in a troubled world and are part of an – at times – confused church, our God is compassionate and faithful, especially in the midst of hopelessness and despair. But our God is also challenging and demanding. God demands that we truly become his people by imitating the example and following the teaching of Jesus his Son. This requires us to reach out to people in need, to care for one another, to try to make the world a better place but, most importantly as Christians, to remain faithful to him who has chosen us to be his people.

It is time, then, to eradicate our strange images of God. So let us pray that we may become more aware of God's loving presence in our lives and that we may have the courage to remain faithful to Christ and his church.

For meditation
I will count you a kingdom of priests, a consecrated nation. (Ex 19:6)

Prayer
God our Father,
we rejoice in the faith that draws us together,
aware that selfishness can drive us apart.
Let your encouragement be our constant strength.
Keep us one in the love that has sealed our lives,
help us to live as one family
the gospel we profess.
We ask this through Christ our Lord.

Twelfth Sunday in Ordinary Time

First reading: Jr 20:10–13

Reflection
Sometimes it is difficult to sustain a committed Christian lifestyle. However, the word of God offers us a timely and welcome message of hope and encouragement as we struggle to practise Christ's teaching. We desperately need such a message in our society, which is characterised by a consumerist mentality, materialistic values, dubious moral options and cynicism.

It has become acceptable – and to some people even commendable – to neglect the challenge of the gospel that Christ entrusted to his church and to abandon our efforts to implement it living and working with others. The message of God's word in a phrase is: do not let others intimidate you from doing what Christ and his church have taught you to know and believe to be true.

We learn much from the Old Testament prophets. In the Book of the Prophet Jeremiah, we read about Jeremiah's consciousness of his unpopularity. People openly displayed animosity towards him and they persecuted him because he had spoken on behalf of God and challenged them to change their lifestyles radically. He encouraged them to live more honestly and with integrity – in conformity with God's plan for them.

In the midst of his unpopularity, Jeremiah remained confident and full of hope, knowing that God was with him in this struggle. With God on his side, anyone else who might be against him could never ultimately succeed. God empowered Jeremiah to be courageous at all times. He knew that God would always be committed to him and would support him.

Jeremiah's courage and conviction provide us with a fundamental and practical message: in this world anyone who speaks the message of God's truth and applies the church's teaching to life's situations and circumstances can expect some form of rejection and persecution. People do not like to admit that sin is a reality in their lives. God's word confronts them with that truth. Often, when they do not like the message, they shoot the messenger. Thus to be prophetic (that is, to speak for God) is costly in terms of our acceptance and popularity.

But God demands that we be prophetic and, thereby, challenge the injustice, immorality, hypocrisy and other sinful practices in our world. We are called to promote Christian values – for example, obedience, humility and charity – by word and example. This can be a very lonely task because it usually means that we are in conflict with those we love in our families and among our friends. It would be much easier in many instances not to disturb the status quo and pretend not to notice inequity, unfairness and wrongdoing.

We need to be convinced, like Jeremiah, that God is always inspiring us to bring his message of salvation and hope to the world. God supports us as we do this and we need to cultivate our ability to trust God, especially when other people ridicule and dismiss us.

For meditation

He has delivered the soul of the needy from the hands of evil men. (Jr 20:13)

Prayer
God of the universe,
we worship you as Lord.
God, ever close to us,
we rejoice to call you Father.
From this world's uncertainty we look to your covenant.
keep us one in your peace, secure in your love.
We ask this through Christ our Lord.

Thirteenth Sunday in Ordinary Time

First reading: 2 K 4:8–11, 14–16

Reflection
In the Second Book of Kings, we read about a Shunammite woman's hospitality to the prophet Elisha (the successor to Elijah), who became a regular visitor to her home. We also read that she was rewarded with a wonderful blessing because of her hospitality. The blessing was undoubtedly beyond all her dreams. Although she was childless and her husband was old, Elisha told her that she would give birth to a son. How incredible this news must have seemed and how overjoyed she must have been when it was revealed to her.

There are at least two important lessons to be learned from this biblical story. First, we are encouraged to be hospitable towards others and especially welcoming towards strangers. They usually bring God's presence into our lives. Secondly, we are invited to be completely open to God's surprises which, in response to our goodness and kindness, often fulfil expectations that were completely beyond our imaginations. These surprises are declarations of God's perfect love.

Hospitality is an admirable virtue that makes a genuine difference to the quality of our relationships with other people. Hospitality was particularly recommended in the Old Testament. At that time the Chosen People were expected to extend a hearty welcome to strangers and to respond generously to their needs, especially to holy people. Later, in the New Testament, Jesus urged his disciples to be generous in their hospitality. For him hospitality was about generosity of spirit. In one of his parables, Jesus said, 'I was a stranger and you made me welcome' (Mt 25:35), suggesting that in welcoming strangers we really welcome Christ himself.

Hospitality is more than simply receiving other people into our homes and being kind to them. It is fundamentally a respectful attitude towards their dignity and a recognition of God's presence in them. It is accepting that, whatever their external appearance and behaviour, all people are made in God's image and likeness. Thus hospitality is essentially about us welcoming and being responsive to God.

It is relatively easy to be hospitable towards those we know and like. However, such hospitality presents no major challenge. It is far more difficult to welcome strangers who are quite different from us culturally, politically, religiously and socially. At present there are many strangers – refugees, asylum seekers and members of the travelling community – in our society, in addition to the homeless and street beggars. Sometimes we treat them badly. Yet, like us, they are all God's children and they deserve our respect and help. They may even bring us a blessing.

God never forgets our welcome of him into our lives. This is invariably manifested in our hospitality towards the various people around us. Just as nine centuries before the birth of Jesus God rewarded the Shunammite woman for her kindness to his prophet, he always rewards our hospitality towards others because, effectively, it demonstrates our welcome of him. God frequently rewards us in ways that we would never have imagined. Therefore, in a spirit of trust, we can be open to God's blessing in whatever way it comes.

Our experience of God teaches us that, if we expect a blessing, we will indeed receive a blessing. Through our hospitality and generosity of spirit, we bring many blessings to other people by welcoming them and, through them, Christ. In return, we are blessed abundantly in our own lives and struggles.

Hospitality is a great virtue. Let us pray that we will be genuinely hospitable people and readily welcome strangers, realising that God comes into our lives through them.

For meditation
Look, I am sure the man who is constantly passing our way must be a holy man of God. (2 K 4:9)

Prayer
Father in heaven,
the light of Jesus
has scattered the darkness of hatred and sin.
Called to that light
we ask for your guidance.
Form our lives in your truth, our hearts in your love.
We ask this through Christ our Lord.

Fourteenth Sunday in Ordinary Time

First reading: Zc 9:9–10

Reflection
The prophet Zechariah, living several centuries before Christ, brought a message of peace and hope to the Jewish people. He told them that, when the Messiah (the Saviour) would come, all wars would end and a kingdom of peace would be inaugurated. Furthermore, the Messiah would bring unity to a divided nation.

Contrary to the people's expectations, the Messiah would be a king whose personality and leadership would be characterised by humility rather than triumphalism and arrogance. Thus he would differ significantly from many of the people's leaders who were often corrupt and uncaring. The Messiah would make a tremendous difference to people's lives if they welcomed him and were willing to be led by him.

Zechariah, speaking on behalf of God, said to the people: 'Rejoice heart and soul, daughter of Zion! Shout with gladness, daughter of Jerusalem! See now, your king comes to you; he is victorious, he is triumphant, humble and riding on a donkey… He will proclaim peace for the nations' (Zc 9:9–10).

These words prefigure Jesus' entry to Jerusalem on Palm Sunday. On that day, the crowds would have willingly made Jesus their king. The people treated him as triumphant, yet he was truly humble – he was carried on a donkey. The crowds loved him because he taught with authority, unlike their own scribes.

Jesus' message was one of peace and unity. However, it is a peace that the world cannot give and a unity that can only be found in God. The peace that Christ came to share is peace of soul, a far deeper peace than any earthly peace and harmony. This peace, in contrast with merely earthly peace, results from living according to the truth that is revealed by Jesus through his words and actions.

During his ministry, Jesus developed the teaching of Zechariah and the other prophets. They had spoken about a gentle and compassionate God and his desire to be close to his people. Jesus went further. God is certainly compassionate towards the repentant sinner and his mercy is endless. But God is also demanding, having high expectations of us. God wants us to be perfect as he is perfect. Ironically, it was the authority with which Jesus taught that made him both loved and hated at the same time.

Unfortunately, after Palm Sunday the crowds quickly changed their minds about Jesus. Within a few days they demanded that he would be crucified. How quickly they forgot their commitment to him. In many respects history was repeating itself.

The message of Zechariah and the other prophets before Jesus had always been rejected, or accepted initially and subsequently abandoned. The people, through their unfaithfulness to God and their sins, continually broke the special (covenant) relationship between God and themselves. Jesus received the same treatment. Sadly, this is another testament to our fallen human nature that we can so easily abandon Jesus, as the crowds who had loved him and followed him when he walked among them on this earth also did.

Zechariah challenges us with several important questions. How willing are we to wait faithfully for the Messiah to come into our lives and activities? When he comes, what can we do to remain loyal to his teaching and example? How can we imitate his humility in our daily lives to demonstrate that we are not corrupt and uncaring towards others?

Let us decide not to let history repeat itself and let us be faithful to the triumphant yet humble Messiah all the days of our lives.

For meditation
See now, your king comes to you; he is victorious, he is triumphant, humble and riding on a donkey. (Zc 9:9)

Prayer
Father,
in the rising of your Son
death gives birth to new life.
The sufferings he endured restored hope to a fallen world.
Let sin never ensnare us
with empty promises of passing joy.
Make us one with you always,
so that our joy may be holy,
and our love may give life.
We ask this through Christ our Lord.

Fifteenth Sunday in Ordinary Time

First reading: Is 55:10–11

Reflection
We usually dislike rainy weather because it causes us inconvenience. We have to button up so that we do not get wet and sometimes we have to remain indoors. We wish that the rain would stop and that the sun would shine continuously. Yet we forget that, without water, the earth could not survive. In particular, plants would die quickly. Their attractive colours and consistent growth depend mainly on the essential moisture provided by rain and snow. In honesty, we must admit that rain and snow are absolutely necessary and powerfully effective in maintaining and enhancing physical life on this earth.

The same can be said about the spiritual effectiveness of God's word. His word may be compared to life-giving water. Just as plants need water, so our souls need to be nourished by God's word and inspired to do God's will. We begin to understand God's will by listening attentively to his word as it is communicated to us through the scriptures and the church's authentic preaching. When we think about God's word, we are thinking about how God has revealed his truth to us.

We receive the message of God's word by reading the scriptures prayerfully and by reflecting seriously on the church's teaching, often in the silence of our hearts. Soon we realise that God's word challenges us to imitate the example of Jesus who was completely open to the Father's will and obedient in all circumstances. Jesus invited his disciples to change their lives radically by abandoning sin and taking up the cross every day. This is what God's word demands from us.

God himself, speaking through the prophet Isaiah, says: 'As the rain and snow come down from the heavens, and do not return without watering the earth, making it yield and giving growth to provide seed for the sower and bread for the eating, so the word that goes from my mouth does not return to me empty, without carrying out my will and succeeding in what it was sent to do' (Is 55:10–11). God is absolutely confident that his word accomplishes much.

Just as rain and snow envelop plants and are soaked up by dry roots seeking life-giving moisture, the word of God nourishes us spirituality with God's truth. Therefore, God's word should be powerfully effective because, coming from God, it is filled with God's life. Therefore, we might well ask: how could it possibly be ineffective?

Unfortunately, however, God's word is often ineffective in our lives – simply because God respects our free will and does not impose his ways on us. God's word can only become effective if we welcome it and allow its influence to change our attitudes and behaviour. Whenever we refuse to accept the truthfulness of God's word and remain unresponsive to its challenges, we are rendering it ineffective. We are like plants whose roots are prevented from soaking up the life-giving water that is all around them. Consequently, there is a real danger that we may die spiritually just as plants may die physically.

Water is a precious gift from God. So also is God's word. We depend completely on God for our existence and God's word is absolutely necessary for our consolation and encouragement. If we are open to God's word, it will achieve wonderful results in our lives. Let us pray, then, that we will not 'button up' spiritually by resenting the inconvenience caused by God's word, thereby excluding God's word and its saving message from our lives.

For meditation
The word that goes from my mouth does not return to me empty, without carrying out my will and succeeding in what it was sent to do. (Is 55:11)

Prayer
Father,
let the light of your truth
guide us to your kingdom
through a world filled with lights contrary to your own.
Christian is the name and the gospel we glory in.
May your love make us what you have called us to be.
We ask this through Christ our Lord.

Sixteenth Sunday in Ordinary Time

First reading: Ws 12:13, 16–19

Reflection
We often have rather naïve images of God, images that simply do not reflect the truth about God. For example, some of us are afraid of God, supposing that he makes life needlessly challenging and miserable. So we live in fear and cannot celebrate the inherent goodness of life. More of us are dismissive of God. We do not really believe that he exists, and we rely on the fact that, if he exists, he loves us anyway regardless of how we behave. Finally,

some of us, while acknowledging God's existence, are convinced that he is impersonal and, at best, quite indifferent towards us.

However, the reality is that God cares about everyone and everything in the world, and is forever merciful. Thus the writer of the Book of Wisdom, referring to God, is able to affirm with confidence: 'There is no god, other than you, who cares for everything … Your justice has its source in strength, your sovereignty over all makes you lenient to all' (Ws 12:13–16).

Throughout the Old Testament, God reminded the Israelites that they were his most prized possession. They were his Chosen People. God was not ruthless and merciless, although he was all-powerful. He was just and lenient, constantly calling his people to repentance whenever they were unfaithful to his commandments. In fact, he loved them so much that he had freed them from the oppression in Egypt. He saved them from the cruelties and humiliations being inflicted by the Egyptians. God chose the Israelites – those whom others would have least expected – to be his own people.

They had countless experiences of God's compassion because it was evident that he had shown them great care. God was both just and merciful. He regularly gave them opportunities to repent and return to him. It emerged that there was no reason to fear God because God was always on their side, if only they could accept this and respond accordingly. However, God expected the people to be faithful and loyal. They were required to obey God's voice and to hold fast to the covenant relationship that he had established with them. Such were the demands that God made as he established an alliance with the Israelites as his people.

We need to remember that, as members of God's people in Christ's church, we are the descendants of the Israelites. Although we live in a troubled and confused world, God is compassionate and faithful, especially in the midst of hopelessness and despair. But God is also challenging and demanding. God demands that we truly become his people by imitating example and living by the teaching of Jesus his Son. This requires us to reach out to people in need, to care for one another, to try to make the world a better place but, most importantly as Christians, to remain faithful to him who has chosen us to be his people.

The true image of God portrayed in the Bible is that he is 'mild in judgement' and that he governs us 'with great lenience' (Ws 12:18). Lord Acton's famous maxim that 'absolute power corrupts absolutely' certainly does not apply to God. Being made in the image and likeness of God, we are challenged to treat other people in the same way that God treats us.

It is time to renew our commitment to the truth about God who is just and merciful. So let us pray that we may become more aware of God's loving presence in our lives and that we may have the courage to remain faithful to the teaching of Christ and his church.

For meditation
After sin you will grant repentance. (Ws 12:19)

Prayer
Father,
let the gift of your life
continue to grow in us,
drawing us from death to faith, hope and love.
Keep us alive in Christ Jesus.
Keep us watchful in prayer
and true to his teaching
until your glory is revealed in us.
Grant this through Christ our Lord.

Seventeenth Sunday in Ordinary Time

First reading: 1 K 3:5, 7–12

Reflection
When I was a child at school, one of my teachers often said 'I would need the wisdom of Solomon to solve that problem' when replying to some of the questions he was asked. At that time, I did not know who Solomon was but I assumed that he must be a very clever and learned man. Many years later, I learned that he

was one of the significant characters in the Old Testament. He was Israel's third king (961–922 BCE approximately), the son of David and Bathsheba.

The basis for the frequently used phrase 'the wisdom of Solomon' is found in the First Book of Kings. There we read that God said to King Solomon in a dream: 'Ask what you would like me to give you' (1 K 3:5). Solomon's response was unusual because, unlike many people, he did not ask for something for himself, for example, a long life, personal wealth, greater power or victory over his enemies. Instead he asked God for the gift of wisdom so that he might wisely rule and lead his people.

Solomon said to God, 'Now, YHWH my God, you have made your servant king in succession to David my father. But I am a very young man, unskilled in leadership. Your servant finds himself in the midst of this people of yours that you have chosen, a people so many its number cannot be counted or reckoned. Give your servant a heart to understand how to discern between good and evil, for who could govern this people of yours that is so great?' (1 K 3:7–9) Basically, Solomon prayed for the gift of wisdom in preference to any other gift.

There is an important message for us in this biblical story: Solomon was not self-centred, and he obviously thought about others before thinking about himself. He wanted the entire people, and not only himself, to benefit from God's gift.

It is crucial to be able to discern the difference between good and evil, right and wrong, when leading people, especially by example. If we do not know the difference ourselves, then how can we possibly hope to explain and teach it to others? As Solomon admitted that he had limitations and asked God to help him overcome them, we need to do the same.

Also, Solomon was humble. He acknowledged that wisdom is a gift from God. Therefore, he did not demand it or presume that he would automatically receive it but asked for it, allowing God to decide whether or not he would share it with Solomon. Thus he recognised God's authority.

How do we recognise God's authority today? We often speak about following the guidance of the Holy Spirit. But how do we know that it is the Holy Spirit and not some other spirit that is influencing us? For Catholics, the answer is simple. We recognise

God's authority in the church's teaching and worship, particularly in the unbroken tradition preserved through the church's Magisterium or teaching office.

Saint Augustine emphasised the link between the church and the Holy Spirit when he said: 'In the measure in which you love the church, in that same measure do you possess the Holy Spirit.' This resonates with Christ's words: 'If you love me, you will keep my commands' (Jn 14:15).

If only we all had the wisdom of Solomon. Significantly, Solomon was commended by the Lord for his humility and concern for others. Let us pray that we will be similarly commended because of our fidelity to God and to the way of life that he has given us through the church.

For meditation
Give your servant a heart to understand how to discern between good and evil. (1 K 3:9)

Prayer
God our Father,
open our eyes to see your hand at work
in the splendour of creation,
in the beauty of human life.
Touched by your hand our world is holy.
Help us to cherish the gifts that surround us,
to share your blessings with our brothers and sisters,
and to experience the joy of life in your presence.
We ask this through Christ our Lord.

Eighteenth Sunday in Ordinary Time

First reading: Is 55:1–3

Reflection
The Book of Isaiah contains many visions about what will happen to God's people when the Messiah comes in the fullness of time.

This is why the visions are often described as messianic or eschatological (that is, to do with the end of chronological time). Through the various visions, God communicates how he will care for and sustain his people and how he will ultimately redeem them and share his eternal life with them.

Among the most incredible visions is God's invitation to a magnificent banquet. The Lord says: 'Oh, come to the water all you who are thirsty; though you have no money come! Buy corn without money, and eat, and, at no cost, wine and milk. Why spend money on what is not bread, your wages on what will fail to satisfy? Listen, listen to me and you will have good things to eat and rich food to enjoy' (Is 55:1–2). Importantly, the Lord continues: 'Pay attention, come to me; listen, and your soul will live' (Is 55:3).

These concluding words indicate clearly that there is a significant difference between this banquet and other meals. It is not just about being offered physical nourishment. It is about sustaining the soul, it is about life with God. Everyone is invited to the banquet of life, and the only expectation of them is a thirst for God.

Although this particular vision in the Book of Isaiah dates from the sixth century before the birth of Christ, when the exiles were in the wilderness returning from Babylon to Israel, for Christians this messianic banquet prefigures the Eucharist. The Eucharist is not just another meal. It is spiritual food for eternal life. Not alone is life promised in the Eucharist; rather, life, God's life in Christ, is freely given. This is the essential difference between the Eucharistic banquet and all other meals.

The Eucharist is an expression of the everlasting covenant referred to in Isaiah's vision: 'With you I will make an everlasting covenant out of the favours promised to David' (Is 55:3). Like the people of the Old Testament who were unfaithful to God's covenant, we are often unfaithful to the covenant that has been established by Christ through his self-giving and self-offering in the Eucharist. He taught his disciples that whoever eats his flesh and drinks his blood will live for ever.

Therefore, Catholics need to examine regularly their attitudes to the Real Presence of Our Lord in the Eucharist. The church teaches us that the Eucharist is the source and summit of its life.

It is a foretaste of the heavenly banquet to which all God's people are invited.

How do we experience our yearning for the Eucharistic presence of Jesus, the Living Bread that has come down from heaven which gives life to the world? In what ways do our reverence for the Blessed Sacrament reflect our Catholic beliefs? For example, do we genuflect whenever in the presence of the Blessed Sacrament and do we receive Holy Communion prayerfully and with reverence? What are the qualities of our lifestyles that are in harmony with the Eucharistic faith we celebrate at Sunday Mass? If our moral lives are obviously incompatible with the church's teaching, we are refusing to be nourished by the Eucharist. We will inevitably discover, as Isaiah warns, that we 'spend money on what is not bread' and our 'wages on what fails to satisfy' (Is 55:2).

Thus we need to be attentive to the prophet's warning, confident that, in doing so, we are responding to God's incredibly generous invitation to enjoy the 'rich food' (Is 55:2) about which Isaiah speaks and that our faith teaches us is Our Lord himself in the sacrament of the Eucharist.

For meditation
Oh, come to the water all you who are thirsty. (Is 55:1)

Prayer
God our Father,
gifts without measure flow from your goodness
to bring us your peace.
Our life is your gift.
Guide our life's journey,
for only your love makes us whole.
Keep us strong in your love.
We ask this through Christ our Lord.

Nineteenth Sunday in Ordinary Time

First reading: 1 K 19:9, 11–13

Reflection

Can we remember some of the occasions when we experienced God? In the First Book of Kings the prophet Elijah, after spending the night in a cave while fleeing through the wilderness, met God in the gentle breeze when he went outside the cave. He encountered God where he least expected and when he was in trouble. (He had incurred the wrath of Jezebel, the wife of King Ahaz, having challenged her pagan practices.)

This seems to be an unexpected way to meet God, especially when we sometimes presume that God is found only in life's dramatic and terrifying events; for example, in a 'mighty wind' or an 'earthquake' or a powerful 'fire', to use the imagery of 1 Kings (19:11–12). However, God is as likely to be experienced in life's insignificant moments and routine happenings. Indeed, Saint Thérèse of Lisieux based her spiritual life on the belief that we please God by doing all our daily tasks as well as we possibly can, offering them to God for our own sanctification and for the salvation of others.

The prophet Elijah was unable to escape from God even in the wilderness because God was (and is) everywhere. Regardless of how we try, we cannot escape from the Living God and his providential care, although we can choose not to have God as part of our lives.

The lesson from Elijah's experience of meeting God in the gentle breeze is that God's ways are not our ways. Too often we want to construct our image of God according to our specification, forgetting that God is the Creator and that we are creatures. We must learn to accept God on God's terms.

God never abandons us. The story about Elijah's encounter with God reminds me of the well-known reflection, *Footprints* (by an unknown author):

> One night a man had a dream. He dreamed he was walking along the beach with the Lord. Across the sky flashed scenes from his life. For each scene, he noticed two sets of footprints in the sand; one belonging to him, and the other to the Lord.

When the last scene of his life flashed before him, he looked back at the footprints in the sand. He noticed that many times along the path of his life there was only one set of footprints. He also noticed that it happened at the very lowest and saddest times in his life.

This really bothered him and he questioned the Lord about it. 'Lord, you said that once I decided to follow you, you'd walk with me all the way. But I have noticed that during the most troublesome times in my life, there is only one set of footprints. I don't understand why, when I needed you most you would leave me.'

The Lord replied, 'My precious, precious child, I love you and I would never leave you. During your times of trial and suffering, when you see only one set of footprints, it was then that I carried you.'

Even when we are unaware of it, God sustains us throughout life's trials and tribulations. God loves and cares for us at all times, even when he may seem far away. God never leaves us, despite what we think and do and say.

Where and when do we encounter God? How do we understand that God's ways are not our ways? Unfortunately we tend to judge God by our own standards, forgetting that our flawed judgements and actions are not reflected in God because God is perfect. Let us pray that we will truly encounter the Living God and be renewed in faith and hope.

For meditation
Stand on the mountain before YHWH. (1 K 19:11)

Prayer
Father,
we come, reborn in the Spirit,
to celebrate our sonship and daughterhood in the Lord Jesus Christ.
Touch our hearts,
help them grow towards the life you have promised.
Touch our lives,
make them signs of your love for all people.
Grant this through Christ our Lord.

Twentieth Sunday in Ordinary Time

First reading: Is 56:1, 6–7

Reflection
Do we believe in the universality of God's salvation? And if we do, is this belief evident in our lives, particularly regarding how we treat the various people we meet every day? These questions are always relevant – especially in the aftermath of the horror induced by terrorist attacks and planted bombs around the world.

After such events, most people are naturally fearful and nervous about using public transport and about being in public places. Understandably, they worry about being victims of attacks. Even so, this does not justify random retaliatory attacks (verbal and physical) on innocent people simply because of their religion and ethnic origin. In our judgements we need to distinguish between condemning the sin and loving the sinner. Consequently, we never generalise about people from other racial and religious backgrounds.

For example, several centuries before the birth of Christ, the prophet Isaiah insisted that God's salvation was not exclusively for the Jewish people. God spoke to them through the prophet. He said: 'Foreigners who have attached themselves to YHWH to serve him and to love his name and be his servants – all who observe the Sabbath, not profaning it, and cling to my covenant – these I will bring to my holy mountain. I will make them joyful in my house of prayer. Their holocausts and their sacrifices will be accepted on my altar, for my house will be called a house of prayer for all the peoples' (Is 56:6–7).

Thus God was stating unambiguously that, contrary to Jewish presumption, other people could and would be saved too. The Jews were the Chosen People but this did not mean that they had a monopoly on salvation. Salvation would indeed come through the Jewish people because the Messiah would emerge from them, but salvation would not be confined to them.

Non-Jews would also share in God's salvation, provided they would serve God, obey his commandments and worship him sincerely. They would be eligible to join the covenant people and they should be respected. Isaiah's message challenged the Jewish people who had returned to the Promised Land from their exile in Babylon because it required them to welcome foreigners. God's love was inclusive.

The truth about the all-inclusive embrace of God's love and the universality of salvation has not changed. God desires that all people will be with him for ever in heaven. But this does not mean that everyone will eventually be in heaven. God has given each one of us the gift of free will. If we freely choose to reject God in this life by sinful attitudes and behaviour, thereby opting to exclude God from our activities and relationships, then God will not force us to accept him in death as we enter the next life. God will judge us accordingly.

However, it is not for us to judge other people especially if their religious beliefs and skin colour are different from ours. Judgement is properly reserved to God alone. Therefore, we need to remind ourselves constantly of the church's mission to bring Christ and his teaching to them with respect and genuine love. As Christians, we cannot be unkind to them, but neither should we deny them the truth of our faith. God's salvation in Christ is for everyone. Let us renew our belief in the all-inclusive quality of God's love and the universality of God's salvation. And let us resolve to spread the name of Jesus and the truth of his saving gospel throughout the world.

For meditation
I will bring [foreigners] to my holy mountain. (Is 56:7)

Prayer
Almighty God, ever-loving Father,
your care extends beyond the boundaries of race and nation
to the hearts of all who live.
May the walls, which prejudice raises between us,
crumble beneath the shadow of your outstretched arm.
We ask this through Christ our Lord.

Twenty-First Sunday in Ordinary Time

First reading: Is 22:19–23

Reflection
In the Book of Isaiah, there is an account of the dismissal from office of Shebna, who was the 'master of the palace' (Is 22:15), for King Hezekiah. (Hezekiah was the king of Judah towards the end of the eighth century before the birth of Christ.) The exact reasons for Shebna's dismissal are not listed. Nevertheless, we can assume that he misused the authority that had been given to him.

For example, he had been planning military alliances between Judah and other smaller nations so that, together, they might engage in a war with Assyria, which was a far more powerful nation. The prophet Isaiah had criticised him for this. At any rate, Shebna was no longer considered worthy to be Hezekiah's representative.

The Lord was unequivocal. He said to Shebna: 'I dismiss you from office, I remove you from your post' (Is 22:19). But that was not all. The Lord continued: 'I call on my servant Eliakim son of Hilkiah' (Is 22:20). Eliakim would succeed Shebna, ensuring that Hezekiah's palace would not be without a senior official.

Also, the Lord foretold that Eliakim would become 'a father to the inhabitants of Jerusalem and to the House of Judah' (Is 22:21). However, most significantly, the Lord indicated that he himself would 'place the key of the House of David on [Eliakim's] shoulder' and that 'should he open, no one shall close, should he close, no one shall open' (Is 22:22).

Prior to Shebna's removal from office, the symbol of his authority was the key that hung from his shoulder. Effectively, Shebna had controlled who entered and departed Hezekiah's household. In future, however, Eliakim would exercise this role, and he would have the authority to open and close the door giving access to the king.

For Catholics in particular, the text from the Book of Isaiah regarding the key assumes a profound importance when it is applied to Jesus. Generally, the giving of a key (or keys) symbolises the granting of authority. This happened when, centuries later, Jesus said to Peter: 'I will give you the keys of the kingdom of heaven; whatever you bind on earth shall be considered bound in heaven; whatever you loose on earth shall be considered loosed in heaven' (Mt 16:19).

Jesus was a descendant of King David. He was – and is – the true Son of David. In promising the keys of the kingdom to Peter, Jesus was telling him that he (and his successors) would exercise a unique office in the church. Thus the gospel text recording Jesus' giving of the keys of the kingdom to Peter is hugely significant, especially in the context of the prophetic text from Isaiah. Jesus' words would have been a clear sign to the apostles, and to Peter himself, that Peter's role in the church would be pivotal.

In addition, Peter (and his successors), in the words spoken by God about Eliakim, would become 'a [spiritual] father to the inhabitants of the [New] Jerusalem' (Is 22:21), the church. This is true of every pope since Peter even if all popes like Peter – and Eliakim before all of them – are imperfect in different ways. Nevertheless, the pope is the spiritual father and leader of all Catholics in the world. He is the Vicar of Christ on earth and we have a duty to be respectful and obedient to him. That is the significance of the symbolism of the keys.

For meditation
I place the key of the House of David on his shoulder. (Is 22:22)

Prayer
Lord our God,
all truth is from you,
and you alone bring oneness of heart.
Give your people the joy
of hearing your word in every sound
and of longing for your presence more than for life itself.
May all the attractions of a changing world
serve only to bring us
the peace of your kingdom which this world does not give.
Grant this through Christ our Lord.

Twenty-Second Sunday in Ordinary Time

First reading: Jr 20:7–9

Reflection

Jeremiah was comparable to other Old Testament prophets regarding the task that God gave him. Like them, he was a reluctant prophet. He did not choose prophecy as a way of life. And yet, in conscience, he realised that he must respond to God's call by doing what God told him, even if it meant being unpopular and that many people would reject him and his message.

Jeremiah was remarkably forthright in his relationship with God and sometimes he became quite angry. He spoke to God from the heart and was not afraid to express his feelings. For example, on one occasion he said: 'I am a daily laughing-stock, everybody's butt. Each time I speak the word, I have to howl and proclaim: "Violence and ruin!" The word of God has meant for me insult, derision, all day long.' (Jr 20:7–8). These were strong words indeed. Jeremiah did not leave God in any doubt as to his thoughts and feelings. Obviously, preaching the word of God was very troublesome and arduous.

However, these words were spoken in the context of other spoken words. Jeremiah also said to God: 'You have seduced me, YHWH, and I have let myself be seduced; you have overpowered me: you were the stronger' (Jr 20:7). Jeremiah was remarkably honest. On the one hand, he was blaming God for inveigling him against his wishes. On the other hand, he was admitting that he freely allowed himself to respond to the prophetic call.

Thus Jeremiah candidly acknowledged the precise nature of his relationship with God. He had yielded to God's will, recognising that he was not on the same level as God who was stronger and greater. Basically, God was the Creator and Jeremiah was the creature. Jeremiah's resistance to God was futile.

In the New Testament, we read about similar incidents involving Jesus and his heavenly Father. Before his arrest in Gethsemane and during his subsequent torture and crucifixion, he prayed: 'My Father, if it is possible let this cup pass me by' (Mt 26:39) and 'My God, my God, why have you deserted me?' (Mt 27:46). Nevertheless, Jesus also prayed: 'Let it be as you, not

I, would have it' (Mt 26:39) and 'Father, into your hands I commend my spirit' (Lk 23:46). Jesus' total trust in his Father far outweighed any doubts.

Both Jeremiah and Jesus were committed to doing God's will, whatever the consequences. This teaches us that fidelity to God's will demands perseverance and discipline. Living according to God's commandments and the church's teaching does not happen naturally.

Because of the effects of Original Sin in our lives, we tend to be selfish and self-centred, easily succumbing to the Devil's temptations. It is far more attractive to be popular with people by compromising our principles than it is to be unpopular because we always speak the truth that often confronts them in their sinfulness.

While God permits our use of free will, whenever the saving message of his word is presented clearly to us there is really no other option but to welcome it and change our lives accordingly. This inevitably involves speaking and being truthful in all our relationships and activities, regardless of the impact that may have on our popularity. But, then, Jeremiah and the other prophets recognised the futility of resisting God. Let us do the same and become prophetic figures in today's world.

For meditation

The word of YHWH has meant for me insult, derision, all day long. (Jr 20:8)

Prayer

Lord God of power and might,
nothing is good which is against your will,
and all is of value which comes from your hand.
Place in our hearts a desire to please you
and fill our minds with insight into love,
so that every thought may grow in wisdom
and all our efforts may be filled with your peace.
We ask this through Christ our Lord.

Twenty-Third Sunday in Ordinary Time

First reading: Ezk 33:7–9

Reflection
How aware are we of our Christian duty to correct other people – always charitably, of course – when they are speaking and behaving badly? Likewise, how do we understand and explain our responsibility to accept, humbly and gratefully, legitimate correction from others when our words have been intemperate and our actions unbecoming of a follower of Christ?

We live in a society where most people choose to ignore the wrongdoings of others because of fear or indifference or the risk of becoming unpopular. Consequently, they do not get involved when they witness family members having rows or co-workers disparaging their colleagues or strangers being verbally and, perhaps, physically attacked on the streets. The attitude of many of us is 'Mind my own business and don't get involved in other people's situations.'

Regrettably, this attitude is dangerously individualistic because it contradicts the reality that God intends us to work together as a pilgrim people, constantly helping, guiding, inspiring and supporting one another. It assumes that we have no responsibility for the conduct of those around us, whereas, in fact, we have a serious God-given duty of stewardship and care.

We have a basic duty to correct others when they are putting their souls in danger by what they are saying and doing. While we are obviously responsible for our own actions, daily life cannot be reduced to merely existing for ourselves with no interest in what other people are saying and doing.

We must work for the common good, remembering that what is necessary for evil to triumph is for good people to say and do nothing. Silence and inaction are never adequate responses to evil and wrongdoing. Whenever people do nothing, it is never subsequently acceptable for them to claim that they did not try to prevent the evil because it was none of their business and they will be held accountable for their lack of action, if not in this life then in the next.

God made this clear when speaking through the prophet Ezekiel. God said: 'When you hear a word from [God's] mouth, warn them in [God's] name. If you do not speak to warn the wicked man to renounce his ways, then he shall die for his sin, but [God] will hold you responsible for his death' (Ezk 33:7–8). In other words, we have an obligation to care for others pastorally, and for the salvation of their souls, by correcting them when necessary. We cannot avoid this obligation which is an obligation arising from Christian charity rather than from self-righteous arrogance.

But we cannot compel other people to listen to us. Our responsibility is primarily to alert them to the truth of God's word and to give them good example. God, again speaking through Ezekiel, said: 'If, however, you do warn a wicked man to renounce his ways and repent, and he does not repent, then he shall die for his sin, but you yourself will have saved your life' (Ezk 33:9).

Just as we are responsible for correcting others when they are wrong, we are similarly obliged to listen to them when they respectfully correct our misguided attitudes and sinful lifestyles. Correction works both ways and is necessary for the integrity of our various relationships. Thus we are personally responsible for our own behaviour but we also have some responsibility for other people.

Christ's final words on this earth commanded his disciples to care for souls by preaching and living his gospel. If others, including our family members, are living a life that is a counter-witness to the gospel because of sin, then we are obliged to tell them. This is true charity. If we fail to do so, we, like them, will be called to account for the scandal. As Ezekiel taught, each one of us is responsible for our neighbours' spiritual welfare.

For meditation
When you hear a word from my mouth, warn them in my name. (Ezk 33:7)

Prayer
Lord our God,
in you justice and mercy meet.
With unparalleled love you have saved us from death
and drawn us into the circle of your life.
Open our eyes to the wonders that life sets before us,

that we may serve you free from fear
and address you as God our Father.
We ask this in the name of Jesus the Lord.

Twenty-Fourth Sunday in Ordinary Time

First reading: Si 27:30 – 28:7

Reflection
Let us reflect on the following two phrases from the word of God in the Old Testament: (a) 'Resentment and anger, these are foul things, and both are found with the sinner' (Si 27:30); and (b) 'Forgive your neighbour the hurt he does you, and when you pray, your sins will be forgiven. If a man nurses anger against another, can he then demand compassion from the Lord? Showing no pity for a man like himself, can he then plead for his own sins?' (Si 28:2–4).

We let these phrases speak to our hearts and souls. What are they saying to us? Do they remind us of Jesus' teaching in the New Testament? When teaching the disciples how to pray, Jesus included the phrase 'And forgive us our debts, as we have forgiven those who are in debt to us' (Mt 6:12). Jesus also said, at the end of the parable about the wicked servant, 'And that is how my heavenly Father will deal with you unless you each forgive your brother [and sister] from your heart' (Mt 18:35).

The first phrase is clear in its meaning: if we are resentful and angry, then we are undoubtedly sinners because of the presence of these sinful characteristics in our lives. Anger linked with resentment is always different from the righteous anger we may sometimes feel when we witness injustice. There is a distinction between the two types of anger.

Most people would not be proud to be known as sinners. Yet many of us do not hesitate to display anger and resentment towards other people, usually because of jealousy and spitefulness. Effectively, we fail to recognise some of the more serious symptoms of our sinful living. The lesson is simple: if we do not want to be sinners, then we cannot bear resentment and anger towards others. We cannot have it both ways.

The second, longer phrase has a similar message. Again, it links anger to sin, but it goes further. We cannot expect God to forgive our sins if we are unwilling to forgive other people for their offences against us and the hurt they have caused us. Thus we cannot operate double standards, whereby we are less demanding on ourselves than on other people.

Basically, then, if people wrong us, we are obliged to forgive them – regardless of how difficult this may be. Otherwise we are wasting our time asking God to forgive us. We must recognises that God does not forgive us on our own terms. Instead, we are challenged to accept God's forgiveness on his terms.

Why does God seem to be so demanding? Having created us, he understands human nature completely. God knows that vengeance and bitterness, and other forms of resentment and anger, eventually succeed in destroying us as individuals and damaging – sometimes irreparably – the communities in which we live and work. Ultimately they rob us of happiness and peace of mind. The only way to avoid such disasters is to cultivate and practise the virtue of forgiveness by forgiving as well as being forgiven.

Frequently, there is a false caricature presented of Catholics as being a guilt-ridden people. However, of all peoples, Catholics have no reason to feel guilty if they celebrate sincerely the sacrament of reconciliation. In that sacrament, our sins are forgiven and the guilt of our sins is wiped away. But we can only experience God's forgiveness if we, in turn, forgive others.

Let us pray the Prayer of Saint Francis every day:

> Lord, make us a channel of your peace. It is in pardoning that we are pardoned, in giving to others that we receive, and in dying that we are born to eternal life. Amen.

For meditation

Forgive your neighbour the hurt he does you, and when you pray, your sins will be forgiven. (Si 28:2)

Prayer
Father in heaven, Creator of all,
look down upon your people in their moments of need,
for you alone are the source of our peace.
Bring us to the dignity which distinguishes the poor in spirit
and show how great is the cause to serve,
that we may share in the peace of Christ
who offered his life in the service of all.
We ask this through Christ our Lord.

Twenty-Fifth Sunday in Ordinary Time

First reading: Is 55:6–9

Reflection
In many respects God, who created the heavens and the earth, is completely different from us and the world. Speaking to the Israelites through the prophet Isaiah, God emphasised the immeasurable dissimilarities by saying: 'My thoughts are not your thoughts, my ways are not your ways – it is YHWH who speaks. Yes, the heavens are as high above the earth as my ways are above your ways, my thoughts above your thoughts' (Is 55:8–9). These words seem to imply that God is utterly remote from us, with no possibility of us ever knowing him and developing a relationship with him.

However, they should be understood in the context of other words spoken by God through Isaiah. Decisively, God also said: 'Seek YHWH while he is still to be found, call to him while he is still near' (Is 55:6). Mysterious words indeed! God, who in one sense is infinitely beyond our reach and transcends our human powers of comprehension, is in another sense close by inviting us to search for and call him. This invitation to seek and call God indicates clearly that it is possible for human beings to have a personal relationship with God. It demonstrates God's great benevolence and generosity towards us.

Relating personally to God demands that we abandon our sinful attitudes and behaviour. Instead, we turn towards God and rejoice in the pity and forgiveness offered to us. This means that we choose to repent for our sins and forgive the people who have wronged us, just as God has forgiven us. We cannot have a meaningful friendship with God while we are living sinful lives because we will never be able to achieve our ultimate purpose, which is to be in heaven with God for ever.

Every invitation requires a response and God's invitation is no different. That invitation is definite and constant. It always asks us to turn to God and undergo conversion so that we really are creatures made in his image and likeness. It is fundamentally an invitation to take refuge in God who readily forgives our sins and draws us ever closer.

On the one hand, we cannot even begin to comprehend God's plan of salvation because God's ways and thoughts are so unknowable. But, on the other hand, we know all about God's plan of salvation because it has been revealed through the prophets especially and, most explicitly, in Jesus Christ who is the Word made flesh and the fullness of God's revelation. Jesus calls us to be his disciples by listening to his teaching, learning from his example and choosing to live accordingly. He is the Messiah about whose future coming Isaiah and the other prophets spoke.

Among the important questions that we need to ask ourselves regularly are: what are the ways we use to respond to God's call? Why might our response combine a sense of wonder at the utterly incomprehensible Mystery of God with a very real experience of being involved in an intimately personal relationship that deepens every day? Are we consciously able to seek God in the circumstances of our everyday lives, knowing that it is in him we find refuge?

For meditation

My thoughts are not your thoughts, my ways are not your ways. (Is 55:8)

Prayer

Father in heaven,
the perfection of justice is found in your love
and all humankind is in need of your law.

Help us to find this love in each other
that justice may be attained
through obedience to your law.
We ask this through Christ our Lord.

Twenty-Sixth Sunday in Ordinary Time

First reading: Ezk 18:25–8

Reflection
People are repeatedly surprised, and sometimes feel aggrieved, when they are confronted by the consequences of their words and actions. It is as if they assumed that their words and behaviour would have no implications for themselves, their relationships and their activities. But life is never that simple. The reality is that everything we say and do has repercussions and we cannot pretend otherwise. We must take personal responsibility for our attitudes and actions.

Yet many of us blame others completely for whatever goes wrong, sometimes oblivious to the fact that we have contributed significantly to the various predicaments in which we find ourselves. Although what other people say and do invariably have implications for us, and while our words and actions certainly influence them, we must accept that we are the masters of our own destiny. Blaming others, while ignoring our own culpability, is futile. We often bring trouble on ourselves. We decide our future.

This is particularly true regarding our relationship with God. God gives us the gifts of life and free will. How we use that free will has serious implications for our ultimate salvation. God communicated this fundamental truth through the prophet Ezekiel by saying, 'When the upright man renounces his integrity to commit sin and dies because of this, he dies because of the evil that he himself has committed. When the sinner renounces sin to become law-abiding and honest, he deserves to live. He has chosen to renounce all his previous sins; he shall certainly live; he shall not die' (Ezk 18:26–8).

The choice, then, for each one of us is clear: life or death, integrity or sin. Integrity and sin are incompatible. If we live sinful lives, by disregarding the teaching of Christ and his church while remaining unrepentant, we cannot hope to be in heaven with God for eternity. Our deliberate choices in this life will result in either life or death in the next life. This is how the consequences of our words and actions will finally confront us.

In death, each one of us will stand before God and will be accountable for our actions and lifestyles, good and bad alike. We will already have judged ourselves and God will not have to do so again. We will have decided our eternal destiny by how we lived on this earth.

However, Ezekiel's message is not confined to what we say and do. It also refers to what we do not say and do not do. Inactivity can be just as sinful as activity. For example, whenever we remain silent about other people's wrongdoing, especially when it has serious consequences for their innocent victims, we compromise our integrity with God and we sin. The word of God constantly challenges us to be prophetic people who will not be afraid to speak the truth in all circumstances.

So what will it be: life or death? Integrity or sin? The choice is ours. We need to learn to stop blaming others, including the church, for the consequences of our freely chosen words and actions. Let us think before we speak and let us reflect carefully before following a particular course of action, realising that there are always consequences to our words and actions for which we must assume personal responsibility and for which we will be accountable.

For meditation

When the sinner renounces sin to become law-abiding and honest, he deserves to live. (Ezk 18:27)

Prayer

Father of our Lord Jesus Christ,
in your unbounded mercy
you have revealed the beauty of your power

through your constant forgiveness of our sins.
May the power of this love be in our hearts
to bring your pardon and your kingdom to all we meet.
We ask this through Christ our Lord.

Twenty-Seventh Sunday in Ordinary Time

First reading: Is 5:1–7

Reflection
The prophet Isaiah told a rather sombre parable that is a metaphor for the persistent indifference of many people towards God and their total lack of response to God's unconditional love. The parable is sometimes called the 'Song of the Vineyard' because it is a ballad about a vineyard and its owner.

The ballad describes the owner's love for and pride in his vineyard. He located it in fertile soil on a hillside and he never ceased tending it. He dug it, clearing it of stones and cultivating it with great care. He planted 'choice vines' (Is 5:2) and did everything that was necessary for it to yield an abundant harvest. Consequently, the conditions for luxuriant growth were ideal. Not surprisingly, then, after his tireless work and patience, he quite rightly expected the vineyard to produce a rich harvest. But this did not happen. All his work was in vain and his hopes were dashed.

Amazingly, only sour grapes were harvested. The return on the owner's investment and work was worthless and he understandably remarked: 'What could I have done for my vineyard that I have not done? I expected it to yield grapes. Why did it yield sour grapes instead?' (Is 5:4). He had exhausted himself and there was no natural explanation for what had happened.

This parable, in which the vineyard owner symbolises God and humankind is symbolised by the vineyard, is a model of God's care of his people and his constant attention to their needs. It is also a model of their ingratitude and unresponsiveness. The parable narrates the story of the relationship between God and the people. It communicates the ongoing reality of their unfaithfulness to the covenant that had been established between God and them. Their profession of love for God was insincere and their ingratitude was astonishing.

Unfortunately, times have not changed. History is repeated and God is still taken for granted by many people today. They do not respond to God's providential and loving care, as evidenced by their sinful lives and their rejection of the teaching of Christ and his church. In this way they are unfaithful to the new and everlasting covenant that has been established through Christ's suffering and death.

Like the vineyard owner in Isaiah's parable, God expects a genuine response from us (as he did from our ancestors) for his many gifts and blessings. Again, like the owner of the vineyard, God's hopes are repeatedly dashed and he could justifiably say: 'What could I have done for my people that I have not done? I sent them my Son who died for their sins and redeemed them. And still they ignore me and refuse to be my people, after all I've done for them.'

The truth about the covenant that God made with humankind is absolute: God has never turned his back on it and has always remained faithful. In contrast, during the course of human history, people – both individually and communally – have been indifferent to the covenant and their responsibilities to God, thereby compromising the covenant relationship. Sadly, we are often similar to the fruitless vineyard. Our lives are characterised by ingratitude and indifference towards God.

We need to learn from Isaiah's parable. The fundamental challenge for each one of us, metaphorically, is to bear much fruit as a sign of grateful appreciation for the life and many opportunities God has given us.

For meditation

Yes, the vineyard of YHWH Sabaoth is the House of Israel. (Is 5:7)

Prayer

Almighty and eternal God,
Father of the world to come,
your goodness is beyond what our spirit can touch

and your strength is more than the mind can bear.
Lead us to seek beyond our reach
and give us the courage to stand beyond your truth.
We ask this through Christ our Lord.

Twenty-Eighth Sunday in Ordinary Time

First reading: Is 25:6–10

Reflection
What, we may ask, will the end of time be like when the reign of God will finally emerge in its fullness? Specifically, how will the kingdom of God in the future differ from our present life in this world? Are there any particular mental images of the afterlife and of how it will happen? And what will eternal life with God be like? These are some of the perennial questions that have preoccupied most believers throughout human history.

While there are no precisely defined answers to these and similar questions, because they ultimately relate to the Mystery of God which is incomprehensible for human beings – what Saint Paul refers to as 'the things that no eye has seen and no ear has heard, things beyond the human mind, all that God has prepared for those who love him' (1 Co 2:9) – there are several insights to be found in the Bible.

For example, eight centuries before the birth of Jesus Christ, the prophet Isaiah shared an eschatological (that is, end-times) vision of a great future for God's Chosen People, and indeed people from every nation, on God's holy mountain, the heavenly Jerusalem.

According to Isaiah, in that future there will be no more tears and mourning because death will have been destroyed and people will have everything they need for true happiness. In the words of Isaiah: 'On this mountain [God] will remove the mourning veil covering all peoples, and the shroud enwrapping all nations, [God] will destroy Death for ever' (Is 25:7–8). Isaiah was reminding his listeners that good times would come for those who trusted God and faithfully kept his law, especially in the midst of hardship and afflictions.

Isaiah described the future in terms of a marvellous heavenly banquet, symbolising eternal happiness, to which God will invite all people. There they will experience the lavishness of God's hospitality and the many blessings of God's benevolence. Again, in Isaiah's words: 'YHWH Sabaoth will prepare for all peoples a banquet of rich food, a banquet of fine wines, of food rich and juicy, of fine strained wines' (Is 25:6). Unfortunately, however, this does not mean that everyone will partake in the banquet. Some people will reject the invitation, a call that leads to heaven, and choose to live sinful lives.

Thus salvation is not to be taken for granted. If people reject God's invitation completely in this life, they will also reject it in death. But all those who accept the invitation will be gathered together as a family in God's presence. And realising that God has saved them they will say: 'See, this is our God in whom we hoped for salvation' (Is 25:9).

The Catholic understanding of the Eucharist is that it is the great eschatological banquet, offering us a foretaste of eternity. The Eucharist is the Body of Christ, the spiritual food that strengthens us on our earthly pilgrimage towards heaven. As we welcome Jesus truly present under the appearance of bread and wine into our lives, allowing him to change us, we grow into his likeness.

Whenever we celebrate the Eucharist, earth unites with heaven and we glimpse in the here and now what life will be like in the future. The Eucharist symbolises and brings about that future intimacy with God and with one another which was promised by God in Isaiah's vision of the heavenly banquet at which all people who die in God's friendship will be guests. This is what eternal life with God will be like. With genuine true faith, let us rejoice and be glad.

For meditation

The Lord YHWH will wipe away the tears from every cheek. (Is 25:8)

Prayer
Father in heaven,
the hand of your loving kindness
powerfully yet gently guides all the moments of our day.
Go before us in our pilgrimage of life,
anticipate our needs and prevent our falling.
Send your Spirit to unite us in faith,
that sharing in your service,
we may rejoice in your presence.
We ask this through Christ our Lord.

Twenty-Ninth Sunday in Ordinary Time

First reading: Is 45:1, 4–6

Reflection
Who or what is the most important reality in our lives? Where and how do we invest most of our time, energy and commitment? Is it in ourselves, with the entire world revolving around us and our particular interests and activities? Perhaps it is in our families, where no one and nothing else matters apart from the happiness and achievements of our spouse and children. Maybe it is in our work, where earning money and making profit have taken control of our lives to the exclusion of everyone and everything else.

However, for people who believe that God is the Creator of the universe, and who specifically believe that Jesus Christ is the Incarnate Son of God, the single most important reality must surely be God and a wholesome relationship with God. This does not imply that people themselves, their families and their prosperity have no value or are unimportant. They are certainly important. But their significance is relative, as it must always be in the context of God who creates and sustains, resulting in an acknowledgement that God is life's most important reality. God is ultimate reality.

Evidence of this is found throughout the Bible, the written record of God's self-communication, in the Old Testament and especially in the Book of Isaiah. The evidence is found even more in the gospels where Jesus often spoke about putting God first. In the Book of Isaiah, God communicates a clear message to King Cyrus. God says to him: 'I am YHWH, unrivalled; there is no other God besides me. Though you do not know me, I arm you that men may know from the rising to the setting of the sun that, apart from me, all is nothing' (Is 45:5–6).

God's words could not have been stronger. During the sixth century before the birth of Christ, these words formed the foundations for the people's faith in one God as distinct from a belief in many gods that was prevalent among neighbouring nations at that time. God was effectively assuring the Israelites during the Babylonian exile that the gods of the Babylonians should not be feared because they did not actually exist. The Israelites needed such encouragement and hope at a time when their faith was being tested severely as a result of their recurring infidelity to God. A succession of prophets had warned them that such infidelity would always lead to disaster culminating in exile from the Promised Land.

God reassured them that, regardless of their exile due to infidelity and the various attacks from enemies, he was the Lord of history and that they would remain his Chosen People. No power, either natural or supernatural, would ever take his place. God would bring them back to their homeland and all would be well again.

The same is true about us living in the twenty-first century. We are often exiled from true friendship with God because of our sinful lives. Nevertheless, God constantly reminds us that we belong to him and that he will lead us back to truthfulness and integrity. If we trust God and remain faithful to his commandments, and if we regularly celebrate God's forgiveness in the sacrament of penance and are spiritually sustained by the Eucharist, we will be able to abandon the many false gods that could otherwise take control of our lives and we will be assured of eternal happiness. Let us always remember that apart from God, all is nothing.

For meditation
I am YHWH, unrivalled; there is no other God besides me. (Is 45:5)

Prayer
Lord our God, Father of all,
you guard us under the shadow of your wings
and search into the depth of our hearts.
Remove the blindness that cannot know you
and relieve the fear that would hide us from your sight.
We ask this through Christ our Lord.

Thirtieth Sunday in Ordinary Time

First reading: Ex 22:20–26

Reflection
The 'Cry of the Poor' is a well-known hymn whose words include:

> I will bless the Lord at all times, his praise ever in my mouth. Let my soul glory in the Lord, for he hears the cry of the poor. Let the lowly hear and be glad; the Lord listens to their pleas. And to hearts broken he is near, for he hears the cry of the poor. Every spirit crushed he will save, will be ransom for their lives. Will be safe shelter for their fears, for he hears the cry of the poor.

This hymn reminds us of the description in the Book of Exodus of the reality of God's compassion for people who were poor (in the broad sense of that term) and vulnerable people. These included widows, orphans, people who are poor and foreigners. Foreigners were especially susceptible to cruelty and maltreatment because, being strangers, they had no civil rights. They were also unfamiliar with Jewish beliefs and practices and so were easily excluded and ignored.

Yet God was absolutely clear in his commandments to the Israelites. There was to be no mistreatment of strangers. Neither was there to be any harshness towards widows and orphans. Furthermore, there must be no usury and extortion in business dealings. Otherwise, God said to them, 'My anger will flare and I shall kill you with the sword, your own wives will be widows, your own children orphans' (Ex 22:23).

Thus the Chosen People were expected to imitate God's kindness and hospitality, particularly towards strangers, remembering that they themselves had been helpless exiles in Egypt.

The most important relationship in the Israelites' lives was the covenant relationship. The covenant demanded faithfulness to the commandments that emphasised love of God and love of neighbour. So there were direct and indirect (that is, through other people) dimensions to people's relationships with God who would judge them according to the mercy they had shown, or not shown, to others.

There is an important teaching in the scriptures that is as relevant nowadays as it was during the Exodus. God does not tolerate negligence towards powerless people in genuine need of help. Real poverty demands that we respond in God's name because God hears the cry of the poor. Intimacy with God is impossible unless we respect all people as being created in God's image and likeness. This is especially applicable to travellers, refugees, asylum seekers and other foreigners who currently live in our country and who are often exploited by employers and assaulted by some of our fellow citizens. Such behaviour can never be condoned.

God always listens to the cry of the poor, although they may not realise it, and will hold each one of us accountable for our attitudes and behaviour towards them. We cannot treat them badly and presume that our relationships with God remain unaffected. Being Christians, we have obligations in justice towards those in our communities who are less fortunate than ourselves. We are duty-bound to share the truth of our faith. But we are challenged also to care for people's basic material needs.

A fundamental question for all of us is: who are the most vulnerable and powerless in our society and in the church (because spiritual deprivation cannot be underestimated) and what can we do to protect them and care for them? Let us remember that God always hears the cry of the poor and demands that we do the same.

For meditation
If he cries to me, I will listen, for I am full of pity. (Ex 22:26)

Prayer
Praised be you, God and Father of our Lord Jesus Christ.
There is no power for good
which does not come from your covenant,
and no promise to hope in
that your love has not offered.
Strengthen our faith to accept your covenant
and give us the love to carry out your command.
We ask this through Christ our Lord.

Thirty-First Sunday in Ordinary Time

First reading: Ml 1:14 – 2:2, 8–10

Reflection
The prophet Malachi, who lived during the fifth century before the birth of Jesus Christ, deplored the Jewish people for their sinfulness, but he was especially scathing in his condemnation of their priests. His comments were absolutely unambiguous and uncompromising.

Speaking on behalf of God, he said to them: 'And now, priests, this warning is for you. If you do not listen, if you do not find it in your heart to glorify my name, says YHWH Sabaoth, I will send the curse on you and curse your very blessing … You have strayed from the way; you have caused many to stumble by your teaching. You have destroyed the covenant of Levi … You have not kept to my paths but have shown partiality in your administration' (Ml 2:1–9). What a devastating judgement on the priests!

The context of Malachi's remarks was the increasingly sinful lifestyles of the Jewish people. After returning to their own land from exile in Babylonia, they were initially very committed to living good and devout lives. They rebuilt the Temple and practised their religious faith with great sincerity. All seemed to be well in their dealings with God. However, they became careless and began to disregard the teaching of the Law and the Prophets.

Part of the explanation for the people's abandonment of the covenant with God was that their priests, who were the religious leaders at that time, did not teach the authentic message of the word of God. But even worse than that, their lives were seriously corrupt and sinful. Thus Malachi castigated them for being unfaithful to their important vocation. Their fundamental task was to mediate between the people and God. Yet they were unworthy to do so because of their hypocrisy and indifference.

Instead of leading the people to God, they were leading them away from God. All their Temple rituals and sacrificial offerings were meaningless. They had lost their awareness of the necessary connection between sacred worship and everyday life.

We believe that the lessons of the word of God are timeless. Thus Malachi's words are surely relevant in today's world and in our church. During recent years, the vast majority of people have been horrified by the shocking revelations of the sexual abuse of innocent children by some priests. While this scandalous and sinful behaviour is rightly condemned by Malachi's warning, there are other ways in which most priests have not been faithful to their calling.

For example, whenever priests are disloyal to the church's teaching, omitting reference to central doctrines in their preaching, they lead people astray and possibly jeopardise the opportunities for salvation. Likewise, if priests' lifestyles are incompatible with their vocation their credibility will be seriously undermined and they are risking their own salvation by their sinfulness. They need to recall the words of Jesus: 'When a man has had a great deal given him, a great deal will be demanded of him; when a man has had a great deal given him on trust, even more will be expected of him' (Lk 12:48).

There are two very obvious challenges in Malachi's words. First, priests have a serious responsibility to be faithful to their vocation and to remain holy and close to God. Secondly, all of us need to pray that our priests will always have the conviction and the courage to do what their calling demands. And we need to correct them when their words and behaviour are incompatible with that calling. We all have a duty to protect and promote the truths of salvation that have been revealed by God and entrusted to the church.

For meditation
You have strayed from the way; you have caused many to stumble by your teaching. (Ml 2:8)

Prayer
Father in heaven, God of power and Lord of mercy,
from whose fullness we have all received,
direct our steps in our everyday efforts.
May the changing moods of the human heart
and the limits which our failings impose on hope
never blind us to you, source of every good.
Faith gives us the promise of peace
and makes known the demands of love.
Remove the selfishness that blurs the vision of faith.
Grant this through Christ our Lord.

Thirty-Second Sunday in Ordinary Time

First reading: Ws 6:12–16

Reflection
The Book of Wisdom was probably the last of the Old Testament books to be written. Its style, which may seem rather strange to contemporary readers, was similar to that of the philosophers of Alexandria who used a very symbolic style of writing. Their influence on Jewish scholars is evident throughout the wisdom

literature of the Hebrew scriptures. This, however, should not disturb the faith of any of us in the divine authorship of sacred scripture. God used human words to record his revelation.

We often assume that wisdom is about human knowledge and intellectual ability and that, consequently, it may be beyond our grasp. But in the biblical sense, wisdom is about sincerity of heart and the search for God. It is seeking the ideal way to think and live. Wisdom is essentially living a truly spiritual life. Wisdom leads us to seek eternal happiness – this is the soul of Christian activity.

In the Book of Wisdom, the concept of wisdom is used to describe what God is like. Interestingly, divine Wisdom is personified as a female character that is gentle and caring. She reaches out to those who seek her, thus symbolising God's search for each human soul even as that person searches for God.

We read in the book: 'Wisdom is bright, and does not grow dim. By those who love her she is readily seen, and found by those who look for her. Quick to anticipate those who desire her, she makes herself known to them. Watch for her early and you will have no trouble; you will find her sitting at your gates' (Ws 6:12–14).

The fundamental message is that God is already here. The truth is that God, who is always caring, finds us before we ever begin looking for him. Wisdom is a gift from God which is available to everyone. This is indeed an encouraging message, particularly when distressed and confused.

However, we also read in the book: 'She [Wisdom] herself walks about looking for those who are worthy of her and graciously shows herself to them as they go' (Ws 6:16). Wisdom is discovered only by those who desire her. She is not acquired passively. Serious thought and reflection are required on our part.

Without denying that salvation is God's gift and that we cannot attain it unaided, the implication is that we have to choose God. We must exercise the free will that God has given us, making a definite decision to seek God and respond accordingly. When creating us, God desired that we would be in heaven for eternity. But to reach our destiny we need to embrace the Wisdom of God.

The only way to do this is to live sincerely by being faithful to God's commandments. Wisdom teaches us the difference between good and evil, between saintliness and sinfulness. She also teaches us to understand the commandments as liberating instead of causing misery and guilt. Thus being faithful in our relationships, being honest in our business dealings and always behaving decently should bring us great joy and fulfilment.

The personification of wisdom in the Old Testament anticipates the Wisdom of God that reveals itself most perfectly in the person of Jesus Christ, the Word made flesh. Jesus cared so much for us that he even offered his life on the cross for the salvation of all people, knowing that not everyone would accept salvation.

Let us be grateful for the Wisdom of God in Christ our Saviour and let us live truly spiritual lives that are characterised by sincerity of heart and the daily search for God – especially in celebrating the sacraments – who finds us even before we begin our search.

For meditation

Wisdom is bright, and does not grow dim. By those who love her she is readily seen, and found by those who look for her. (Ws 6:12)

Prayer

Almighty Father,
strong is your justice and great is your mercy.
Protect us in the burdens and challenges of life.
Shield our minds from the distortion of pride
and enfold our desire with the beauty of truth.
Help us to become more aware of our loving design
so that we may more willingly give our lives in service to all.
We ask this through Christ our Lord.

Thirty-Third Sunday in Ordinary Time

First reading: Pr 31:10–13, 19–20, 30–31

Reflection
The Book of Proverbs presents the Old Testament description of the perfect wife and asks: who can find her? According to the description, the perfect wife 'is far beyond the price of pearls. Her husband's heart has confidence in her ... She is always busy ... she does her work with eager hands ... She holds out her hand to the poor, she opens her arms to the needy' (Pr 31:10–20). In addition, her wisdom is more important than her charm and beauty.

Many people today regard this description of a wife as outdated. Nevertheless, because it refers to what is deepest in human nature, there are important practical lessons to be learned from it. To help us appreciate its value, we need to remember the context in which it was written. The wisdom literature in the Old Testament understood life very much from a male perspective. Not surprisingly, then, one of God's most sought-after blessings for a wise man was the gift of an excellent wife.

The ideal wife possessed an abundance of those virtues towards which the wise man aspired. Because of her virtues, she was close to God and could help her husband to get closer to God. Thus the husband who was married to a good wife considered himself to be truly blessed by God. In this way man and woman complemented each other, as God planned, rather than competed with each other.

Applying the description of the perfect wife to ourselves, regardless of whether we are men or women, married or single, we can learn much. For example, we can be busy doing the work that God has asked us to do. This work mainly involves being faithful to the teaching of Christ and his church, allowing it to inspire our attitudes and motivate our behaviour, both at home and at work or school. This is how we cultivate virtues to overcome our selfishness.

We must be enthusiastic about sharing our faith with others – that is our baptismal duty. Just as in Proverbs, the perfect wife could enable her husband to become closer to God because of her own holiness, by our good example we too can encourage other people to deepen their commitment to God. We have a duty to challenge them to abandon their sinful lifestyles and seek the peace of mind and heart that only God can give.

Many of us have more than we need to live comfortably in the material sense. Hence there is no legitimate reason why we cannot be generous with our material wealth and share some of it with those who are less fortunate than us. We need to remember that we will always have the poor with us. Treating them properly and respectfully, always attending to their spiritual needs, will help us attain salvation.

The perfect wife is really an example of the perfect Christian. The same question could be asked about the perfect Christian as about the perfect wife: who can find him/her? Long after Proverbs was written, Jesus summarised his moral teaching by saying to his disciples: 'You must therefore be perfect just as your heavenly Father is perfect' (Mt 5:48). Adherence to Christ's commandments is how the perfect Christian is recognisable.

The Little Flower (Saint Thérèse of Lisieux) once said that it is not the extraordinary things that we do in life that matter, but the ordinary things that we do extraordinarily well. That could have been the motto of the perfect wife described in Proverbs and it could be the motto for any of us seeking to become perfect Christians.

For meditation

A perfect wife – who can find her? (Pr 31:10)

Prayer

Father in heaven,
ever-living source of all that is good,
from the beginning of time you promised human beings salvation
through the future coming of your Son, our Lord Jesus Christ.
Help us to drink of his truth
and expand our hearts with the joy of his promises,
so that we may serve you in faith and love
and know for ever the joy of your presence.
We ask this through Christ our Lord.

Our Lord Jesus Christ, Universal King

First reading: Ezk 34:11–12, 15–17

Reflection
The Feast of Christ the King, which is the last feast of the liturgical year, was instituted by Pope Pius XI in 1925. Although the image of a king is central to the feast, its purpose is not to be triumphalist, although it celebrates Christ's victory over evil and worldliness. Jesus is referred to as King because he inaugurated the kingdom of God here on earth. But, as King of every nation, he is a servant king, a humble king who offered his life for his people. Whenever we imitate his humility we are pleasing to God.

The prophet Ezekiel provided a helpful image for understanding the kingship of Jesus. Ezekiel shared a wonderful message from God with the people of his time. Through the prophet, God – using the imagery of a shepherd tending his flock – said: 'I am going to look after my flock myself and keep all of it in view … I shall rescue them from wherever they have been scattered during the mist and darkness … I myself will pasture my sheep, I myself will show them where to rest' (Ezk 34:11–12, 15).

The imagery, which may seem strange to us but which was very familiar to the Jewish people, and its message are obvious. God himself would lead and guard his people. They would no longer be entrusted to religious leaders who had guided them so badly in the past. Unlike those false shepherds, God would remain faithful and never lead them astray. God's love was personal and individual and, at the same time, communal. The communal response to God consisted of the combined responses of individuals. Thus the people as a whole, in addition to the individuals, were important.

Speaking specifically about the lost sheep, God said, 'I shall look for the lost one, bring back the stray, bandage the wounded and make the weak strong … I shall be a true shepherd to them' (Ezk 34:16). With these words God was effectively promising his people that he would return them to the land from which they had been scattered. He would care especially for those who, mostly in the spiritual sense, were lost or wounded or weak.

But this did not suggest that God would ignore those people who had remained faithful to the commandments. God would love and protect everyone who allowed him into their hearts and souls. God was referring to the false shepherds who had led people astray spiritually by putting material realities before spiritual realities.

The people appreciated the significance of the shepherd image because it was powerfully evocative for them. Good shepherds were unlike indifferent herdsmen. They were always concerned for every sheep and even risked their lives to protect them. Much of the misfortune experienced by the Israelites had arisen from their corrupt leaders who were bad shepherds. God would rectify the mistakes of the past and ensure a better future.

Taking the image of the good shepherd and applying it to Jesus, the essential message of the Feast of Christ the King is that God cares. God loves us so much that he sent his only Son so that everyone who would believe in him would gain eternal life. The question for us on this great feast is: do we trust sufficiently in God's providential care? In other words, do we allow ourselves to be guided and challenged by the teaching of Christ and his church so that we will be happy with God for ever in heaven after our lives on this earth have ended?

We thank God for Jesus the Good Shepherd and we pray for good and holy bishops who, imitating Christ, will be courageous and tireless preachers of the gospel truths in every situation.

For meditation
I am going to look after my flock myself and keep all of it in view. (Ezk 34:11)

Prayer
Father all-powerful, God of love,
you have raised our Lord Jesus Christ from death to life,
resplendent in glory as King of creation.
Open our hearts,
free all the world to rejoice in his peace,
to glory in his justice, to live in his love.
Bring all humankind together in Jesus Christ your Son,
whose kingdom is with you and the Holy Spirit,
one God, for ever and ever.

Glossary

Advent: From the Latin *adventus* which means coming. The liturgical season that prepares to commemorate the first coming of Christ at Christmas and anticipate his Second Coming at the end of time.

Anointing of the sick: One of the seven sacraments of the church, celebrated with people who are seriously ill, weakened by illness, in danger of death or burdened by old age.

Apostasy: A 'falling away'. Usually a deliberate and complete abandonment of the faith previously held.

Apostles: Messengers or ambassadors of the Good News.

Ark of the Covenant: A chest described in the Book of Exodus as containing the tablets of stone on which the Ten Commandments were inscribed.

Ascension: The glorified and victorious return of the risen Jesus to heaven, where he intercedes for us and exercises his power over the entire universe.

Ash Wednesday: The first day of Lent, characterised by a penitential service during which the faithful receive ashes (from burned palms) – a symbol of the human need for repentance – on their foreheads.

Baptism: One of the three sacraments of Christian initiation, in which water is applied to a person by immersion or pouring.

Bible: A collection of seventy-three sacred books (in the Catholic version) written by numerous authors who were inspired by God.

Blessing: In the Christian understanding, an authoritative declaration, invocation or bestowal of divine approval and grace, usually accompanied by the sign of the cross.

Charity / Love: The greatest of the three theological virtues. Charity enables people to love God and their fellow human beings unselfishly.

Chosen People: The people chosen to be in a covenant relationship with God.

Christmas: The liturgical season observed as commemorating the birth of Christ.

Church: Those who are true believers in Christ. The term is used in the New Testament both in a universal sense (all such believers) and in a restricted sense (a particular group of believers gathered in one place).

Confirmation: One of the three sacraments of Christian initiation in which the recipient consciously and intentionally confirms or ratifies the faith testified to in baptism.

Conscience: The sense of being obligated to do the right and avoid the wrong.

Conversion: In the Christian sense, the act of a person in turning to Christ. It includes repentance (renunciation of sin) and faith (acceptance of Christ).

Corporal works of mercy: Virtuous human actions inspired and motivated by one's love of God and related to the physical or bodily needs of human beings.

Covenant: In the Judaeo-Christian sense, an agreement between god and humankind in which God pledges to bless those who accept and commit themselves to him.

Creator: A reference to God in terms of his having brought into existence all that is.

Creature: Any being that derives its existence from God.

Devil: Satan: the supreme evil spiritual being, who rebelled against God and now is engaged in opposing him. In the last times, the Devil will be finally subdued.

Disciples: In the Christian sense, a learner or follower of Jesus.

Easter: The liturgical season during which the resurrection of Christ is celebrated.

Epiphany: The liturgical feast of manifestation of the divinity in Jesus of Nazareth.

Eschatology: The study of the last things.

Eternal: Having neither beginning nor end.

Eucharist: One of the seven sacraments.

Faith: One of the three theological virtues. Belief in and commitment to something or someone. Christian faith is specifically a complete trust in Christ and his saving work as the basis of one's relationship with God.

Fallen human nature: The human race in its condition after the Fall (Original Sin).

Five Books of Moses: The Pentateuch, the first five books of the Bible – Genesis, Exodus, Leviticus, Numbers and Deuteronomy.

Forgiveness: In the Christian sense, pardon of sin. God practises forgiveness and also expects his followers to do so.

Free will: The concept that human choices and actions are self-determined. It has been used as a solution to the problem of evil: evil is understood as resulting from human misuse of the freedom God gave.

Gentile: One who is not by race a Jew.

Godparents: Those who accept the important role of caring for a child's on-going spiritual welfare if the child's parents cannot do so.

Golden Rule: One should treat others as one would like others to treat oneself.

Good News: The gospel.

Gospel: The message of salvation offered by God to all who believe; also, one of the first four books of the New Testament, which recount the life and teachings of Jesus.

Grace: God's dealing with human beings in undeserved ways; it is simply an outflow of God's life, goodness and generosity.

Heaven: The future abode of believers. A place of complete happiness and joy, it is distinguished especially by the presence of God.

Hebrews: The earliest name for Abraham and his descendants.

Hell: The place of future punishment of wicked persons; it is a place of great anguish from which God is totally absent.

Historical Jesus: The person of Jesus as he lived on earth and can be investigated by the methods of historical research. The historical Jesus contrasts with the Christ of faith.

Holiness: A condition of purity or freedom from sin or of being set apart to special service. The imitation of God.

Hope: One of the three theological virtues. The expectation of good things in the future; in the Christian sense, faith regarding the matters that are yet to be.

Humility: The quality of not regarding oneself more highly than one should nor being excessively concerned about one's welfare or reputation.

Immanuel: Literally, 'God with us'.

Incarnation: A reference to the doctrine that the Second Person of the Trinity without giving up his deity became a human being.

Jew: Either a person of Hebrew descent or a practising adherent of Judaism.

Kingdom of God: The reign of God, whether internally within the heart of human beings or externally.

Last Judgement: The evaluation of individuals which will occur in the end times after the return of Christ.

Lectionary: A book that contains a collection of scripture readings designated for worship on a given day or occasion.

Lent: The period of forty fast days (i.e. forty weekdays or forty-six calendar days) from Ash Wednesday to the Saturday immediately preceding Easter. It is intended to be a time of abstinence, prayer and charitable works.

Liturgical year: The several important seasons of the year as determined by the church. Beginning with Advent, certain dates are designated for observance of importance events and truths of the Christian faith.

Love/Charity: One of the supreme attributes of God – concern for and action to bring about the welfare of another.

Magisterium: The teaching authority of the church.

Marriage: One of the seven sacraments of the church. Through this sacrament, a man and a woman are united as husband and wife.

Martyr: Originally, one who gives witness to religious truth; in the later sense of the term, one who seals that testimony with death.

Mercy: Compassion; pardon; forgiveness.

Messiah: Literally, 'the anointed one'. The leader chosen and appointed by God to undertake the special mission of redemption and liberation.

New Testament: The collection of biblical books which the church accepts as God's authoritative revelation about the life of Christ and the mission of the church.

Old Testament: The collection of biblical books which were gathered by the Jews and were generally recognised at the time of Christ as being authoritative.

Omnipotent: The ability to do all things that are proper objects of power.

Omniscient: The ability to know all things that are proper objects of knowledge.

Original Sin: The effect of the sin of our predecessors, and particularly of Adam, upon us. Affecting our behaviour independent of and prior to any action of our own, Original Sin may include both corruption of human nature and guilt.

Pagan: Those who do not acknowledge the one true God.

Paschal Mystery: The suffering, death, resurrection and ascension of Christ – commemorated at the celebration of the Eucharist.

Passover: The initiatory event of the Exodus, when the angel of death took the firstborn of the families of Egypt but spared the firstborn of the people of Israel, who had marked their doorposts with blood. The event is still commemorated by Jews.

Predestination: Being elected for salvation through the eternal foreknowledge and will of God.

Promised Land: The land of Palestine, which God had promised to his people of Israel.

Prophet: One who speaks forth on behalf of God.

Providence: In the Christian sense, God's care for the creation, involving his preserving it in existence and guiding it to his intended goals.

Purgatory: In Catholic theology, a place to which persons go upon death who are neither sufficiently holy to go directly to heaven, nor sufficiently evil to be permanently assigned to hell. Through a process of purging experiences, they will be prepared for heaven.

Real Presence: In the Eucharist, Jesus is literally and wholly present – Body and Blood, Soul and Divinity – under the appearances of bread and wine.

Redemption: Christ's delivering us from punishment by paying the penalty for our sins.

Repentance: In the Christian sense, sorrow for one's sin and a resolve to turn away from it.

Resurrection: The historical event and doctrine of Christ's coming back to life on the third day following his crucifixion.

Revelation: God's free and loving self-communication, especially through Jesus of Nazareth but also in many other ways – through creation, through human history, through other human beings and cultures, and through God's own words and deeds directed toward the spiritual well-being and salvation of all of humanity.

Sabbath: The day of rest and worship. Jews observe it on Saturday, most Christians on Sunday.

Sacrament: A sacred, visible sign of God's presence that brings about what it signifies by manifesting the faith of the church and through which God's free gift of grace is offered.

Salvation: The divine act of delivering a believer from the power and curse of sin and then restoring that individual to the communion with God for which human beings were originally intended.

Salvation history: The whole story of human beings and their world understood as a drama of redemption running from creation to the Second Coming and finding its centre in Christ.

Scripture: Literally, 'writing'. In the Christian sense, the canonically books of the Old and New Testaments.

Second Coming: The return of Christ in glory at the end of history to judge the world.

Sermon on the Mount: Jesus' discourse in Matthew 5–7. It is frequently thought of as the highest of standards for Christian living.

Sin: Any act, attitude or disposition which fails to fulfil completely or measure up to the standards of God's righteousness. It may involve an actual transgression of God's law or failure to live up to his norms.

Soul: The immaterial or spiritual aspect of the human being.

Suffering servant: God's suffering servant. The Jewish understanding is that the suffering servant is the nation of Israel, whereas the Christian understanding is that the suffering servant prefigures the ministry of Jesus.

Synagogue: Jewish place of worship. The first one was probably established during the Babylonian exile.

Temple: Structure erected in Jerusalem for worship of God. Unlike the Tabernacle, which was temporary and portable, the Temple was a permanent house of worship. The first Temple was constructed under the leadership of King Solomon.

Tradition: A set of beliefs and practices passed on from one generation to another.

Transubstantiation: The change, through the Eucharistic words of consecration, of the substance of bread and wine into the Body and Blood of Christ, with the appearances of bread and wine remaining.

YHWH: Transliteration of the proper name by which the God of Israel is known. It is customary when reading or speaking, as a sign of profound reverence, not to pronounce the sacred name YHWH; 'the Lord' is the most commonly used substitution.

Appendix

Biblical Book	Reference	Sunday
Acts	Ac 1:12–14	Seventh Sunday of Easter
	Ac 2:1–11	Pentecost Sunday – Mass during the Day
	Ac 2:14, 22–33	Third Sunday of Easter
	Ac 2:14, 36–41	Fourth Sunday of Easter
	Ac 2:42–7	Second Sunday of Easter
	Ac 6:1–17	Fifth Sunday of Easter
	Ac 8:5–8, 14–17	Sixth Sunday of Easter
	Ac 10:34, 37–43	Easter Sunday – Mass of the Day
Deuteronomy	Dt 11:18, 26–8, 32	Ninth Sunday in Ordinary Time
Exodus	Ex 17:3–7	Third Sunday of Lent
	Ex 19:2–6	Eleventh Sunday in Ordinary Time
	Ex 22:20–6	Thirtieth Sunday in Ordinary Time
	Ex 34:4–6, 8–9	The Most Holy Trinity
Ezekiel	Ezk 18:25–8	Twenty-Sixth Sunday in Ordinary Time
	Ezk 33:7–9	Twenty-Third Sunday in Ordinary Time
	Ezk 34:11–12, 15–17	Our Lord Jesus Christ, Universal King
	Ezk 37:12–14	Fifth Sunday of Lent
Genesis	Gn 2:7–9; 3:1–7	First Sunday of Lent
	Gn 12:1–4	Second Sunday of Lent
Hosea	Ho 6:3–6	Tenth Sunday in Ordinary Time
Isaiah	Is 2:1–5	First Sunday of Advent
	Is 5:1–7	Twenty-Seventh Sunday in Ordinary Time
	Is 7:10–14	Fourth Sunday of Advent
	Is 8:23 – 9:3	Third Sunday in Ordinary Time
	Is 11:1–10	Second Sunday of Advent
	Is 22:19–23	Twenty-First Sunday in Ordinary Time
	Is 25:6–10	Twenty-Eighth Sunday in Ordinary Time
	Is 35:1–6, 10	Third Sunday of Advent
	Is 42:1–4, 6–7	The Baptism of the Lord
	Is 45:1, 4–6	Twenty-Ninth Sunday in Ordinary Time
	Is 49:3, 5–6	Second Sunday in Ordinary Time
	Is 49:14–15	Eighth Sunday in Ordinary Time
	Is 50:4–7	Passion Sunday (Palm Sunday)
	Is 55:1–3	Eighteenth Sunday in Ordinary Time
	Is 55:6–9	Twenty-Fifth Sunday in Ordinary Time
	Is 55:10–11	Fifteenth Sunday in Ordinary Time
	Is 56:1, 6–7	Twentieth Sunday in Ordinary Time
	Is 58:7–10	Fifth Sunday in Ordinary Time
Jeremiah	Jr 20:7–9	Twenty-Second Sunday in Ordinary Time
	Jr 20:10–13	Twelfth Sunday in Ordinary Time

1 Kings	1 K 3:5, 7–12 1 K 19:9, 11–13	Seventeenth Sunday in Ordinary Time Nineteenth Sunday in Ordinary Time
2 Kings	2 K 4:8–11, 14–16	Thirteenth Sunday in Ordinary Time
Leviticus	Lv 19:1–2, 17–18	Seventh Sunday in Ordinary Time
Malachi	Ml 1:14 – 2:2, 8–10	Thirty-First Sunday in Ordinary Time
Proverbs	Pr 31:10–13, 19–20, 30–1	Thirty-Third Sunday in Ordinary Time
1 Samuel	1 S 16:1, 6–7, 10–13	Fourth Sunday of Lent
Ecclesiasticus (Sirach)	Si 3:2–6, 12–14 Si 15:15–20 Si 24:1–2, 8–12 Si 27:30 – 28:7	The Holy Family of Jesus, Mary and Joseph Sixth Sunday in Ordinary Time Second Sunday after Christmas Twenty-Fourth Sunday in Ordinary Time
Wisdom	Ws 6:12–16 Ws 12:13, 16–19	Thirty-Second Sunday in Ordinary Time Sixteenth Sunday in Ordinary Time
Zechariah	Zc 9:9–10	Fourteenth Sunday in Ordinary Time
Zephaniah	Zp 2:3; 3:12–13	Fourth Sunday in Ordinary Time